Greenhouse Gardening For Beginners

The Step By Step Guide For Growing Organic Vegetables, Fruits and Herbs All Year Round.

Table Of Contents

Chapter One: Types Of Greenhouses

Structure design

Greenhouses are available in various shapes and size suitable for multiple climatic zones prevailing on the planet. Each zone requires different forms for giving favorable capable climatic conditions to the development of plants. The greatest amount of insulation possible, covering of maximum ground area for the least cost and a structurally sound facility are some of the criteria for development of several types of greenhouse. From numerous greenhouse designs found for example, is solarium ("lean-to", joined to a house), even and uneven span, "hillside" and saw tooth types are as yet found all through the world. A portion of these are economically impractical and would not meet the necessities of a controlled situation; the sawtooth, be that as it may, has been used in horticulture industry of created nations. The designs showed next are accepted by both European and American guidelines for greenhouse development. Present-day designs have followed from these first methodologies. Unsupported green-houses are usually of two types, peak rooftop (A-frame) or Arch/curvilinear. These designs are bolstered independent from anyone else; for example, no outer support is given. Arch rooftop designs are created not in view of light transmission contemplations, however because of financial elements; these can be built for approximately 25% less expensive than a peak rooftop design. The Arched rooftop is effectively versatile to both unbending and adaptable covering material.

Now and again the unattached peak or Arch designs are joined to frame "frame and wrinkle" office or multi-length. This sort of arrangement is appropriate to the majority of the business greenhouses utilized for horticulture and vegetable creation. They are more affordable to assemble, monitor ground territory, and require less heating expense per ground region contrasted with remain solitary designs (Kacira).

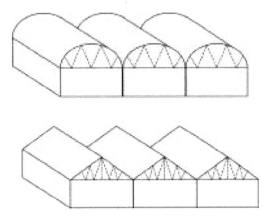

Ridge and Furrow Configuration of Greenhouse Structures.

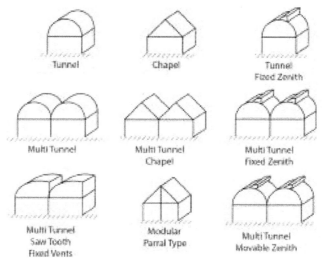

Greenhouse Structure Designs based on Mexican Standard.

Greenhouse confirmation as per Mexican Standard NMX-E-255-CNCP-2008

The greenhouse structure designs, as indicated by the Mexican standard, are given above. Note that the contrast of the mark from the above mentioned yet the geometric shapes are the equivalent; a portion of these designs include a zenith or rooftop vent for accomplishing better ventilation.

Designs description

There are some greenhouse classifications as indicated by various criteria (for example, material for development, spread material sort, rooftop highlights, and so forth.). In any case, it is liked to list the most significant overlooking a few features for classification. Among the most well-known kind of greenhouses on the planet are (Bouzo and Gariglio, 2009):

Arch rooftop – or tunnel, it is portrayed by the state of its housing and its all-metal structure. The utilization of this kind of greenhouse is spreading because of its more prominent capacity to control the miniaturized scale atmosphere, its protection from high breezes and fast establishment with pre-assembled designs. The sections are aroused iron funnels dispersed 5 m 8m or 3 m 5 m separated. The most extreme tallness of such greenhouses is between 3.5 m and 5 m. Side dividers receive statures from 2.5 m to 4 m. The width of these greenhouses is between 6 m and 9 m, and they permit a multi-range arrangement. Ventilation is through horizontal and rooftop windows.

Advantages:

High transmittance of daylight.

Great indoor air volume (high heat latency). Great protection from winds.

Thoroughly free inside space, giving simple uprooting, automated culturing, crops driving, and so forth.

Development of medium to low unpredictability (because of the accessibility of prefabricated components).

Disadvantages:

Significant expense.

They face ventilation challenges in the event that they are worked in multi-length, and there is no rooftop vent system.

Standard peak – or house of prayer, is perhaps the most established design, utilized in constrained harvest cultivation. The incline of the rooftop is variable as indicated by radiation and precipitation (typically changing somewhere in the range of 15∘ and 35∘). Width measurements vary somewhere in the range of 6 and 12 m (considerably higher) for variable length. The stature of the horizontal range between 2.0 m to 2.5 m and 3.0 m to 3.5 m the frame (likewise constructed lower than those shown, however, are not suggested). The ventilation of these greenhouses in a single range has no troubles, turning out to be progressively troublesome when these are canal associated.

Advantages:

Development of low to medium unpredictability.

Utilization of cheap materials relying upon the territory (eucalyptus shafts and timbers, pine, and so on.).

• Side ventilation is exceptionally simple. It is likewise simple to introduce rooftop windows.

• Suitable for both covering materials adaptable and unbending.

• It has incredible offices for depleting water.

Disadvantages:

• Ventilation issues with canal associated greenhouses.

• It has less encased volume than bent greenhouses with a similar peak stature.

• A larger number of components that decrease light transmittance (more noteworthy concealing).

• Internal bolster components thwart the development and area of crops.

Sawtooth – A variety of chapel greenhouses, which was first utilized in quite a while with exceptionally low precipitation and significant levels of radiation were greenhouses that had a solitary rooftop tilted at points going from 5° to 15°. The sidelong coupling of such started the greenhouses known as "sawtooth". The need to clear water from precipitation decided a tendency in assortment zones from the centre towards the two finishes.

Advantages:

• Construction of medium multifaceted nature.

• Excellent ventilation which varies from the multi-length house of prayer greenhouses.

• Use of suitable materials relying upon the region.

Disadvantages:

- Concealing a lot more noteworthy than a chapel because of the more prominent number of supporting basic components.
- Low volume of air encased (for a similar peak stature) than a house of prayer.

Modular Parral type – These greenhouses are originated in the region of Almería (Spain), made up of posts and wires called "parral" which are a changed form of the designs used to develop table grapevines. Right now, there is a cutting frame rendition of the first worked with aroused channels as indoor backings, the utilization of posts stay for horizontal strain holding wind loads. These greenhouses, for the most part, have an frame stature of 3.0 m to 3.5 m, the width is variable, extending inside 20 m or additionally relying upon the length. The slant is practically nonexistent, or in territories with a high water hazard, ordinarily is between 10° to 15°, which speaks to sidelong tallness of about 2.0 m to 2.3 m. It is vented uniquely through horizontal openings.

Advantages:

• Low-cost development.

• Large volume of air encased (great conduct contingent upon the heat dormancy).

• Negligible rate of rooftop components in the block attempt of light.

• High wind load obstruction.

Detriments:

Poor ventilation.

Serious danger of breakage by overwhelming precipitation because of the low seepage limit. Development of high unpredictability (requires specific staff).

In zones of low radiation, the low slanted rooftop speaks to the low take-up of daylight.

Venlo house – These are glass greenhouses where the boards lay on the water assortment channels; they are commonly utilized in Northern Europe. The width of every module is 3.2 m, and the dispersing between posts the longitudinal way is around 3 m. These greenhouses have no side windows (perhaps in light of the fact that in Holland there are very few requests for ventilation). Instead, it has rooftop windows, opening substituting (coordinated side and by the other) whose measurements are 1.5 m long and 0.8 m wide.

Advantages:

The better heat exhibition because of the kind of material utilized: glass, and unbending materials as of now.

• High level of control of natural conditions.

Detriments:

Significant expense.

The transmittance is influenced, not on account of the spread material, however by the enormous number of supporting components because of the heaviness of the spread material. Being an inflexible material, enduring quite a long while, their light transmission is influenced by dust, green growth, and so on.

Greenhouse plan by the atmosphere

Not all greenhouses are planned equivalent. A plan that functions admirably in a cool atmosphere with long virus winters, snowfall, low light and high breezes won't be the best design for a sticky, tropical atmosphere with variable light force. Various greenhouses are described by the degree of insurance from the outside condition they can offer and the ability they can give producers to control within condition to a particular arrangement of shapes. The degree of protection required relies upon the kind of crop being developed and the neighbourhood atmosphere. The target with building any greenhouse is to discover a plan that will permit the producer to defeat the most restricting climatic issues in their specific zone and acquire the greatest development rates conceivable from their crops. The necessities of greenhouse designs because of various climatic zones that can be found the world over are (Morgan, 2012):

Dry tropical or desert atmospheres – The principle ecological dangers are high breezes vehicle drying residue or sand, which can impact the two harvests and greenhouses. Basic tents with shafts developed with high-tractable steel wires to shape an essential design over which a solitary layer of fine creepy-crawly work is extended and verified around the frames. Moist can be expanded by hazing or clouding, which likewise acts to diminish temperatures. Further developed hello there tech, PC controlled and cooled designs are additionally being used in atmospheres like this.

Subtropical desert and Mediterranean atmospheres – A design that can be heated yet at the same time keep up a cool situation in summer are fundamental. Right now atmosphere an appropriate design is the "cushion and fan" cooled plastic greenhouse with top vents and heating. Alongside concealing over the outside of the greenhouse, this creates a perfect domain during dry summer conditions.

Moist tropical atmospheres – Good tropical greenhouse designs can be as straightforward as a downpour spread or plastic rooftop with open or move upsides secured with bug work. In bigger greenhouses, the design is best planned with a "saw tooth" rooftop format which permits great venting of the sight-seeing inside the greenhouse on crisp mornings. Heating, what's more, protection isn't required, and vents can stay open. Moistening systems and air-development fans can be utilized to cool the earth inside this sort of design, and portable heat screens can be utilized to decrease approaching daylight on brilliant, cloudless days and pulled back to permit greatest light entrance under cloudy conditions. High breezes from tropical storms or sea tempests can be a significant hazard right now.

Mild atmospheres – Efficient heating of the air inside the greenhouse and protecting and keeping up this heated air is the primary thought. Cultivators need all year high development rates and most extreme crops in these situations usually select greenhouses highlighting completely clad side dividers, rooftop and side vents, permitting enormous ventilation regions and PC control of ecological equipment, for example, heaters, shade or heat screens, hazing and vents. Mild zone greenhouse designs regularly utilize plastic cladding "twin skins" where the space between the two layers of plastic is expanded, offering improved protection and better natural control.

Cold calm atmospheres – Greenhouses for this sort of condition need strong dividers and firmly built, relatively soak strong rooftops to convey snow stacks that would fall plastic film designs. These greenhouses are frequently twofold protected by introducing plastic film within dividers and situating retractable heat screens over the overhang at stud stature. To forestall heat misfortune, vents are frequently kept shut throughout the winter months.

The world agro-climatic zones show the most appropriate greenhouse design designs, considering the above data.

Most present-day hydroponic greenhouses for all atmospheres nowadays highlight a stud stature of at any rate 3.05 m and at times considerably more. Despite the sort or plan of the greenhouse or what harvest is being grown, a tall greenhouse design gives a superior situation for plants and a bigger cushion against minor changes in outside temperatures. The subsequently improved limit with regards to air development is a fundamental part of present-day greenhouse editing that has been showed to profit various crops by improving transpiration and decreasing malady. The volume of air that should be heated in cooler atmospheres can be diminished by pulling heat screens over the greenhouse rooftop around evening time and heating just under the screen, this makes an enormous protection layer over the screen and under the greenhouse rooftop, along these lines easing back the pace of Heat misfortune through the cladding (Morgan, 2012).

For improved harvest creation and quality, a cautious choice of greenhouse design, coating, and atmosphere control system is required. All greenhouses ought to be planned appropriately to withstand all conceivable burden factors for security and legitimate functionality purposes. The National Greenhouse Manufacturers Association (NGMA) distributes principles that give direction for deciding design loads for greenhouses (Kacira, 2013).

Chapter Two: Materials Economics And Efficient Designs

A greenhouse is designed in such a way that it can be verified that it doesn't surpass the load limits at any time. This is resolved by the sort of greenhouse and the materials utilized. For a keen greenhouse containing high worth equipment and crops, they ought not to be intended for an actual existence cycle under 10 years.

As to strength, it has been established that the insurance against corrosion must not harm the design uprightness at any rate during the greenhouse life-cycle.

The most widely recognized materials utilized for the design, cladding and floor are:

Design materials

There are various frame types being utilized to build greenhouses. Contingent on the necessities, some are better than others.

Galvanized Steel– Mechanical properties of high protection from stresses. It can withstand the surge of both wet and incredibly dry atmospheres—guarantees structural integrity against natural disasters, high-speed winds. Normally greenhouses whose design is made of this material use polyethene or glass claddings.

Wood – Low expense and flexibility. The Types of wood most utilized are pine and maple. Steel and wood designs have solid establishments to guarantee foundations structural integrity against natural disasters.

Low Carbon Steel AISI 1010 – Mechanical properties fundamentally the same as those of galvanized steel. It is less expensive, and it has less environmental effect than stirred steel. Galvanized steel has chemical protection which makes it increasingly durable when uncovered.

High-Strength Low-Alloy HSLA 340 – It has mechanical properties that favour the greenhouse auxiliary honesty. It is utilized in certain cylinders, bases and joints of the design just as screws and nails. Not prescribed for use in farming creation territories. Low toughness contrasted with Galvanized Steel.

Aluminum – It is extremely light and helpful in many modern procedures. Not used to manufacture designs due to having inadequate protection from stresses. It is fitting to use close to places where nourishment is delivered.

Cladding materials

Greenhouse designs generally shift with the kind of greenhouse being the head decision confronting cultivators. The cladding will radically influence the measure of daylight coming to the harvest. The cladding will likewise decide heat loss of the design. The most widely recognized materials are Low-Density Polyethylene (PE) – Low expense. Impervious to outrageous climate conditions, shaping capacity, and it is light; subsequently, it doesn't cause enormous loads on the design. Not promptly degradable so its utilization must be estimated. PE film just keeps going around 2 years. Clear PE is utilized for developing most plants, yet white PE can be utilized to lessen light and heat for growing lowlight plants or for spread.

Glass – The Regular greenhouse is covering against which all others are judged. Great quality glass is an appealing, extremely straightforward, and formal (in appearance) covering material. Significant expense. It isn't as pliable and flexible as polyethene. It is heavier so the design would be dependent upon more prominent Disadvantages. For use in non-forceful conditions because of its delicacy.

Polyvinyl Chloride PVC – The most affordable and utilized decision. Broadly utilized because of its flexibility, pliability and mechanical properties. It is light pressure, so it doesn't create huge worries in the design. Not ecologically benevolent, slow to corrupt.

Vinyl Sheet – Heavier than polyethene, progressively sturdy and extensively increasingly expensive. Whenever made with an ultra-violet inhibitor, it can keep going up to five years. Likewise, similar to polyethene, it has electrostatic properties that pull in dust, which mists the sheeting and along these lines chops down the transmission of light.

Polyester – The most popular polyester film is mylar. In the 5-mm thickness utilized for greenhouses, it has the upsides of being light pressure, sufficiently able to oppose harm by hail, it is unaffected by extraordinary temperatures and has light-transmission attributes very like glass. Mylar is, notwithstanding, costly. It won't be so compelling when utilized on ineffectively fabricated frame s that are shaken by the wind.

Fiberglass Reinforced Panels FRPs – Rigid plastic boards produced using acrylic or polycarbonate that comes in large ridged or level sheets. They are solid, hold heat superior to anything glass does, and are lightPressure. The best bit of leeway of fibreglass is its exceptionally high protection from breakage, implies it should last somewhere in the range of 10 and 15 years. These boards are particularly alluring where light power is high.

Acrylic Semi-Rigid – Usually level acrylic boards are perfect for greenhouses due to their quality, light Pressure, protection from daylight and great light-transmission roast acteristics.

They do scratch effectively, yet separated from this their chief burden is their significant expense. Be that as it may, acrylic merits the expense as it will give great help for a long time.

Floor materials

An establishment is one of the most significant pieces of the greenhouse. Regardless of where the establishment lies, it must be level and square. The materials of greenhouse floors extend from exposed ground to concrete, and various Examples are:

Standard Concrete – Regular solid will suffer around 2500 pounds for each square inch. This blend is fitting for overwhelming Disadvantages, for example, soil-blending regions and areas in the greenhouse where substantial equipment is utilized.

Permeable Concrete – Allows waste forestalling puddling and still gives an obstruction to weed control. Appropriately restored permeable solid will have an ability to persevere through 600 pounds for every square inch of surface. A four-inch floor of this blend will enough persevere through light equipment and faculty.

Rock or Dirt Floors – They are suitable yet frequently not worth the underlying reserve funds. Floors will be mud with visit water systems and will commonly seem unsuitable. Truth be told, these sloppy and temperamental floors are an issue regarding the expense and contamination to the degree that they have incited the quest for substitutes looking like eco-materials.

Eco-materials

A portion of the materials utilized for building a greenhouse couldn't be condition amicable because of their extensive stretch of debasement initiating air contamination. Eco-materials seem to deal with this circumstance, and these are the materials which join less ecological Pressure underway with high recyclability and acknowlframe frame increasingly compelling use of material. Materials ought to be inviting not exclusively to nature yet additionally to humankind.

Eco-materials can allude to the materials utilized for the life-cycle item configuration created so as to ensure nature. There are seven components of eco-effectiveness, for example,

• Reducing the material necessities for merchandise and ventures.

• Reducing the vitality power of merchandise and ventures.

• Reducing dangerous scattering.

• Enhancing material recyclability.

• Maximizing manageable utilization of inexhaustible assets.

• Extending item sturdiness.

• Increasing the administration power of merchandise and ventures.

The eco-materials can be arranged into four primary classes:

• Non-straight source materials.

• Materials for biology and natural insurance.

• Materials for society and human wellbeing.

• Materials for vitality dependent on two primary criteria as their sources and capacities.

Various Examples for eco-materials appear in the following rundown. As it tends to be seen, multiple mixes of eco-materials may serve for the greenhouse design and floor in future advancements.

Greenhouses are required to permit high light transmittance, low Heat consumption, adequate ventilation effectiveness, satisfactory auxiliary quality and great by and large mechanical conduct, low development and working expenses.

Greenhouses are designed considering security, usefulness, general structural respectability and appropriateness. The area, size and casing plan of the greenhouse decides the kind of material and design to be utilized during the development of the greenhouse. The parts of greenhouse designs; posts, frames, belts, and downspouts. The greenhouses' backbone could be made of glass, whose strategic to tie down the spread to ensure the crop. Other than assurance, they bolster any heaps, for example, wind, downpour, day off, water system offices staking, to forestall issues like an invasion, negligible shade during the day, and decrease the issue of daily temperature drops (typically climate). The ventilation, the shape and the material of the greenhouse (which will be portrayed right now) elements to be considered. Mention that the strength of the greenhouse isn't just founded on the materials it is worked of, yet in addition on its plan. Among thought are the designs utilized, the worries to which the gatherings submit (there must be pressure and no pressure), the supports of these designs ought to be longitudinal and extraneous to balance the horizontal power of the breeze, and have great grapple roofing materials, and so forth. In regard to creating loads because of the water system,

refrigeration and different types of equipment, these ought not to be beneath 15 kg/m2. When staking crops over-Disadvantages of 14–16 kg/m2 ought to be considered.

In view of these necessities, principles have been made that look at binding together the design, the development and the creation of greenhouses; in Mexico, this is the NMX-E-255-CNCP-2008 standard, in Europe the UNE-EN13031-1 and in American the standard (ANSI A 58.1-1972) that is given by the National Greenhouse Manufacturers Association (NGMA).

In view of the need of having greenhouses for an ideal crop, right now depiction of the most widely recognized utilized materials to construct the design of the greenhouse will be introduced, just as spreads and the kind of material required to put on the ground to make the establishments (FAO, 2002, Service 2012). There is additional data about eco-materials, which are currently getting all the more financially and ecologically attainable in greenhouses. Also, there is an investigation of the mechanical properties of the materials utilized in greenhouses. This data is furnished with the point of deciding the conduct that the electrifying steel has under certain breeze paces and along these lines to foresee if the material is a decent decision to fabricate a greenhouse.

Design materials

Utilizing the best possible kind of material to build a design is significant for the versatility and effectiveness of the completed item. Brutal climate conditions (day off, hail, wind or sweltering climate) are the most widely recognized reason for the disappointment of greenhouse designs.

The design ought to have the option to take all the fundamental types of Disadvantages; dead, live, wind and day off. The establishment, sections and brackets are designd as needs are. The principle loads, which must be considered in the greenhouse configuration, are (Elsner et al., 2000):

1. Dead burden or lasting burden.

2. Imposed Disadvantages (crop loads).

3. Installations.

4. Snow burden.

5. Wind burden.

6. Seismic burden.

This arrangement depends on the estimation of the lifetime of the greenhouse from the monetary and specialized perspective.
To stay away from basic harms, stress cutoff points ought to be considered, which are associated with a design breakdown imperilling human life (Muñoz et al., 2002). A definitive

point of confinement states, which may require thought, are the accompanying: loss of balance of the design and loss of burden-bearing limit because of breakage, precariousness, weakness, exorbitant strains and disfigurements.

Notwithstanding the kind of material utilized, as far as possible will be dissected mechanically in a plane design, which is a lot of discrete components associated with one another in an inflexible manner, which is intended to withstand the outside powers applied and transmit them to the establishment, without which there would be an over the top breakage or disfigurement of the material.

There are a few frame types being utilized to build greenhouses. Contingent on the necessities, some of them are superior to other people (Juárez-López et al., 2011, Kumar Jaypuria 2008, Yuste Pérez 2008):

Stirred Steel: Has mechanical properties of high obstruction.

• Advantages:

It can oppose both the harm of damp and very dry atmospheres.

It guarantees auxiliary honesty because of cataclysmic events, for example, rapid breezes.

The rooftop is simpler to be worked in an adjusted shape or in a sharp Arch (house of prayer formed like).

It very well may be utilized with polyethene coatings or glass.

• Disadvantages:

High expense.

*Should be evaded in the event that it is at all conceivable the contact of the film with the basic components heated by sun powered radiation.

Wood: The pine and maple are the most regularly utilized, joined with steel cylinders and establishments of concrete or cement to guarantee their basic honesty if there should be an occurrence of normal stun of incredible power.

• Advantages:

A wood outline gives common protection to the greenhouse.

The wood ingests the beams of the sun during the day and holds in the Heat around evening time.

• Disadvantages:

It might be expected to get the wood forestall wood spoil, and the synthetics out-gassing from the pre-treated wood can be dangerous to the plants that are become inside the greenhouse.

Low carbon steel (AISI 1010): Contains less carbon than different steels and is a lot simpler to cold-design because of their delicate and bendable nature.

• Advantages:

Less expensive than the stirred steel. Less effect on nature

• Disadvantages:

It is neither remotely weak nor bendable because of its low carbon content. It has lower elasticity and is pliable.

High-quality, low compound Steel (HSLA 340): The steels in the HSLA extent are appropriate for basic parts. Since they, by and large, have lower carbon than the SS steels, their pliability is prevalent.

• Advantages:

It is prescribed to be utilized in certain channels and in the establishments.

It is prescribed to be utilized in some fundamental intersections of the design just as in the screws and nails.

• Disadvantages:

Try not to utilize a material, for example, this in regions where there is planted land or horticultural creation as it can't be left outside for quite a while.

Aluminium: Round or square tubing is utilized, contingent upon the covering material to be utilized on it.

• Advantage:

It is a solid material and won't rust, and is lightPressure. Boring openings in it is genuinely simple.

• Disadvantage:

Fibreglass boards or polycarbonate sheets could be affixed to the design. As far as basic materials, around half of the greenhouses have metallic designs, 30% is made of wood, and the rest is of blended designs, comprehended as the joined utilization of covered wood, metallic profiles, and so on.

All materials are acceptable when coordinated to the size, shape and area of the completed greenhouse design and the most satisfactory design will be the best to maintain a strategic distance from unexpected temperature changes and permit incredible ventilation. In other words, it will give the best states of development.

Chapter Three: Greenhouse Step By Step Heating/Cooling

Greenhouses ought to give a controlled situation to plant creation with adequate daylight, temperature and stickiness. Greenhouses need the presentation to the most extreme light, especially in the first part of the day hours. Consider the area of existing trees and designs while picking your greenhouse site. Water, fuel and power make natural controls conceivable that are basic for positive outcomes. Hence, utilize solid heating, cooling and ventilation. Cautioning gadgets may be attractive for use in the event of intensity disappointment or if there should be an occurrence of outrageous temperatures.

The house temperature necessities rely on which plants are to be developed. Most plants need during the day temperatures of 70 to 80 degrees F, with night temperatures to some degree lower. Relative stickiness may likewise require some control, contingent upon the plants refined.

A few plants develop best in cool greenhouses with night temperatures of 50 degrees F after they are transplanted from the seeding plate. These plants incorporate azalea, daisy, carnation, aster, beet, calendula, camellia, carrot, cineraria, cyclamen, cymbidium orchid, lettuce, pansy, parsley, primrose, radish, snapdragon, sweet pea and many sheet material plants.

A few plants develop best in heat greenhouses with night temperatures of 65 degrees F. These plants incorporate rose, tomato, poinsettia, lily, hyacinth, cattle orchid, gloxinia, geranium, greenhouse, daffodil, chrysanthemum, coleus, Christmas desert flora, calla, caladium, begonia, African violet, amaryllis and tulip.

Tropical plants, for the most part, develop best in high dampness with night temperatures of 70 degrees F.

Heating

Georgia greenhouses must be heated for all year crop creation. A decent heating system is one of the most significant strides to effective plant creation. Any heating system that gives uniform temperature control without discharging material unsafe to the plants is worthy. Appropriate vitality sources incorporate gaseous petrol, LP gas, fuel oil, wood and power. The expense and accessibility of these sources will shift to some degree, starting with one zone then onto the next. Comfort, speculation and working expenses are largely further contemplations. Reserve funds in labour could legitimize a progressively costly heating system with programmed controls.

Greenhouse heater prerequisites rely on the measure of Heat misfortune from the design. Heat misfortune from a greenhouse, as a rule, happens by every one of the three methods of heat move: conduction, convection and radiation. Generally, numerous types of heat trade happen all the while. The Heat interest for a greenhouse is ordinarily determined by consolidating each of the three misfortunes as a coefficient in a Heat misfortune condition.

Conduction

Heat is led either through a substance or between objects by direct physical contact. The pace of conduction between two items relies upon the region, way length, temperature distinction and physical properties of the substance(s, (for example, thickness). Heat move by conduction is most effectively diminished by supplanting a material that behaviours heat quickly with a poor heat conductor (separator) or by setting an encasing in the Heat stream way. A case of this would supplant the metal handle of a kitchen skillet with a wooden handle or protecting the metal handle by covering it with wood. Air is an exceptionally poor heat conductor and in this manner a decent Heat protector.

Convection

Convection heat move is the physical development of a heat gas or fluid to a colder area. Heat misfortunes by convection inside the greenhouse happen through ventilation and penetration (fans and air spills).

Heat move by convection incorporates the development of air as well as the development of water fume. At the point when water in the greenhouse dissipates, it assimilates vitality. At the point when water fume consolidates back to a fluid, it discharges energy. So when water fume gathers on the outside of an article, it releases vitality to the outside condition.

Radiation

Radiation heat move happens between two bodies without direct contact or the requirement for a medium, for example, air. Light and heat radiation follows a straight line and is either reflected, transmitted or assimilated after striking an item. Brilliant vitality must be ingested to be changed over to heat.

All articles discharge heat every which way as brilliant vitality. The pace of radiation heat move fluctuates with the zone of an item, and temperature and surface attributes of the two bodies included.

Brilliant Heat misfortunes from an item can be diminished by encompassing the article with a profoundly intelligent, misty hindrance. Such a boundary (1) mirrors the brilliant vitality back to its source, (2) retains next to no radiation, so it doesn't heat up, and re-emanate vitality to outside articles, and (3) keeps objects from "seeing" one another, a vital component for brilliant vitality trade to happen.

Elements Affecting Heat Loss

Heat misfortune via air invasion relies upon the age, condition and sort of greenhouse. More established greenhouses or those in poor condition, for the most part, have broken around entryways or gaps in covering material through which a lot of cold air may enter.

Greenhouses secured with enormous sheets of coating materials, huge sheets of fiberglass or a solitary or twofold layer of inflexible or adaptable plastic have less invasion.

The greenhouse ventilation system, likewise, largely affects invasion. Bay and outlet fan shades regularly permit a huge air trade if they don't close firmly because of poor design, soil, harm or absence of grease. Window vents seal superior to anything bay screens, yet even they expect support to guarantee a tight seal when shut.

Sun-powered radiation enters a greenhouse and is consumed by plants, soil and greenhouse installations. The heat articles then re-emanate this vitality outward. The measure of brilliant Heat misfortune relies upon the sort of coating, encompassing temperature and measure of overcast spread. Unbending plastic and glass materials display the "greenhouse impact" since they permit under 4 per cent of the heat radiation to go back through to the outside.

Heat Loss Calculations

Heat misfortune by conduction might be evaluated with the accompanying condition:

$Q = A (T_i - T_o)/R$

Where:

Q = Heat misfortune, BTU/hr

A = Area of greenhouse surface, sq ft

R = Resistance to heat stream (an attribute of the material)

(T_i-T_o) = Air temperature contrasts among inside and outside

Table 1 records various materials regularly utilized in greenhouse development and their related R esteems. Table 1 additionally records in general R esteems for different development congregations. Note that high R esteems show less Heat stream. Building materials that retain dampness will direct Heat once they are wet. Use fume hindrances to secure materials that are porous to water fume. Heat is likewise lost to the ground underneath and adjacent to a greenhouse. The border heat misfortune might be added to different misfortunes utilizing Table 1 and the condition:

$Q = PL (T_i - T_o)$

P = Perimeter heat misfortune coefficient, BTU/ft ºF hr

L = Distance around border

Table 1. Heat Pass-Through Various Construction Materials and Assemblies.

Materials	R-Value
Glass fibreboard, 1"	4.0
Extended polystyrene, 1", cut surfaces	4.0
Extended polystyrene, 1", smooth skin surface	5.0
Extended polystyrene, formed dabs, 1"	3.6
Extended polyurethane, 1"	6.2
Vermiculite, 1"	2.2
Glass fibre cover, 3-3.5"	11.0
Glass fibre cover, 5.0-6.5"	19.0
Divider Materials	
Solid square, 8"	2.00*
Compressed wood, ½"	1.43*
Concrete poured, 6"	1.25*
Solid square or compressed wood, in addition to 1" frothed urethane	7.69*
or on the other hand in addition to 1" polystyrene	5.0*
Greenhouse with slim heat curtains	1.42-3.33*

Development Assemblies

Material	Overall R-Value
Rooftop and Wall Coverings	
Glass, single layer	0.91*
Glass, twofold layer, ¼" space	2.00*
Polyethene or other films, single layer	0.83*
Polyethene or other films, twofold layer separated	1.43*
Polyethene film, twofold layer, isolated, over glass	2.00*
Fibreglass strengthened pane	0.83*
Twofold acrylic or polycarbonate	2.00*
Perimeter	Btu/straight ft ºF hr
Uninsulated	0.8
Insulated	0.4

*Includes impacts of surface coefficients.

Add penetration heat misfortunes to the conduction heat misfortunes. The condition for the penetration of heat move:

$$Q = 0.02 \, V \, C \, (Ti - To)$$

V= Greenhouse volume, cu ft

C = Quant of air trades every hour

Table 2. records evaluations of air trades through Types of greenhouses. The number of air trades every hour will change contingent upon the sort and state of the greenhouse and the measure of wind.

Table 2. Normal Air Exchanges for Greenhouses

Development System	Air Exchanges per Hour1
New Construction, glass or fibreglass 0.75 to 1	
New Construction, twofold layer plastic film	0.5 to 1.0

| Old Construction glass, great maintenance | 1 to 2 |
| Old Construction glass, poor condition | 2 to 4 |

1Low breeze or assurance from wind lessens the air conversion scale.

Minimum Design Temperatures

A decent outside temperature to use in radiator design counts (to choose heater size) can be found by subtracting 15 degrees F from the normal day by day Minimum January temperature (see Table 3). Another prerequisite the radiator must meet is to give enough Heat to keep plants from freezing during times of incredibly low temperatures. The base temperatures for different areas inside Georgia likewise appear in Table 3.

Table 3. Climatic Conditions in Georgia (1948-2004)

Location	Minimum Temperature ºF and (Year Occurring)	Average Daily Minimum January Temperatures (ºF)
Atlanta	-8 (1985)	33.6
Athens	-4 (1985)	33.2
Augusta	-1 (1985)	33.6
Columbus	-2 (1985)	36.4
Macon	-6 (1985)	35.8
Rome	-9 (1985)	30.5
Savannah	3 (1985)	39.0
Tifton	0 (1985)	38.0
Valdosta	9 (1981)	38.6

Example:

Keep up a temperature of 65 degrees F inside a twofold layer plastic greenhouse with measurements as showed in Figure 3 with no establishment protection. Expect an Augusta area.

Surface Area:

Walls   7 x 100 x 2   =   1400.0 ft²

Roof	16.86* x 100 x 2	=	3372.0 ft²
Ends	(32 x 7 + 5.33 x 16)2	=	618.6 ft²
			5390.6 ft²

* This measurement can be controlled by drawing the greenhouse cross-segment to scale and estimating this length along the rafters.

At an Augusta area and a normal every day Minimum January temperature of 33.6 degrees F, the planned temperature would be about 18.6 degrees F, so utilize 20 degrees F. This requires a 45-degree F ascend above plan temperature; and, with twofold layer plastic, the R-worth will be 1.43.

Conduction Heat Loss, QC: = Area x ΔT/R

$$= 5391.0 \times 45/1.43$$

$$= 169,647 \text{ BTU/hr}$$

Volume: = (7 x 32 x 100) + (16 x 5.33 x 100)

$$= 22,400 + 8,528$$

$$= 30,928 \text{ ft}^3$$

Air Infiltration Losses, QA: = 0.02 x Volume x C x ΔT

$$= 0.02 \times 30,928 \times 1.0 \times 45$$

$$= 27,835 \text{ BTU/hr}$$

Border Heat Loss, QP: = P x L x (ΔT)

$$= 0.8 \times 264 \times 45$$

$$= 9,504 \text{ BTU/hr}$$

Absolute Heat Loss, QT: = QC + QA + QP

$$= 169,647 + 27,835 + 9,504$$

Heat Required = 206,986 BTU/hr

The coldest temperature recorded in Augusta is - 1 degree F and, with a 45-degree F temperature rise, the plants ought not to be in peril from freezing. An expansion in heat prerequisite of roughly 20 per cent would be fundamental if the house were situated on a breezy hillside.

Other Heating System Design Considerations

Plastic greenhouses frequently have a stickiness development inside the fenced-in area since basically no breaks or openings exist as in a glasshouse. High moistness can prompt expanded event of leaf and blossom illnesses. A constrained air heating system helps blend the air inside the house and forestalls temperature variety inside the house. Actually, it is alluring to have fans along the dividers to circle and blend the heat air in with the cooler air close to the surface. They can be worked consistently during cold periods regardless of whether the radiator isn't on.

Pipe systems to equitably disperse the heated air from the constrained heat air heater are alluring. At Minimum, two little heating units are desirable over one bigger unit, since two units offer more assurance in the event that one unit breakdowns.

An admonition gadget is adequate protection should the heating system glitch or if a force disappointment happens. Some greenhouse administrators want to have a battery fueled caution system to caution them if the temperature escapes the adequate range.

Ventilation

Ventilation diminishes inside temperature during radiant days and supplies carbon dioxide, which is fundamental to the plants' photosynthesis. Another preferred position of ventilation is to expel heat, wet air and supplant it with drier air. High dampness is frightful since it causes dampness buildup on cool surfaces and will in general increment the event of sicknesses.

Some glasshouses are ventilated by physically worked ventilators in the rooftop. This strategy is typically not acceptable for ventilating plastic secured houses because of the quick temperature variances conceivable. Ventilating fans are energetically prescribed in Georgia.

Winter ventilation ought to be intended to forestall cold drafts on plants. This has been an issue with certain systems utilizing screens toward one side of a house and an exhaust fan at the other. The issue can be limited by setting the admission high in the peak and utilizing perplexes to avoid the approaching air.

Sans draft winter ventilation can be given by utilizing the convection tube system, comprising of Exhaust fans and outside air bays situated in the peak and end divider. This is associated with a slim plastic cylinder expanding the length of the greenhouse. The cylinder is suspended on a wire close to the frame and has gaps along its whole length. The fans can be thermostatically controlled. Fan activity creates a slight gaseous tension drop inside the greenhouse, making outside wind current into the delta and expand the cylinder, which releases air into the house through the openings in the cylinder. The openings emanate "planes" of air that should extend on a level plane to furnish legitimate conveyance and blending in with heat air before arriving at the plants.

The indoor regulator stops the fans when the ideal temperature is come to; the cylinder breakdown and ventilation stops. In a firmly built greenhouse, it has a little effect where fans are situated in convection tube ventilation since the air conveyance is dictated by the cylinders. Less fan limit is typically required for the convection tube system than for some other winter ventilation system. Extra air is vital as the outdoor temperature ascends to where the full limit of the cylinder. The outside air is generally heat enough at this point to be conceded through entryways or different openings at the plant level.

Fans might be included or conceivably joined with a cooling cushion for use in evaporative cooling. Truth be told, air might be gotten through the cushion with or without water in the cushion. In heat periods, enough air should be pulled from the house to give a total air trade like clockwork—control fans by an indoor regulator or humidistat to provide appropriate temperature and mugginess.

Greenhouses furnished with an evaporative cooling cushion system having three fans or less ought to have one fan with a two-speed engine to forestall inordinate temperature changes and fan cycling. Select all fans to work against a slight Pressure (⅛ inch static water pressure). Fans not appraised against slight Pressure, as a rule, move just 60 to 70 per cent of the evaluated wind current when introduced in greenhouses. It is suggested that solitary fans that have been tried and their exhibition checked by an autonomous testing lab, for example, AMCA, be utilized since that is the main affirmation that the design ventilation rate is being accomplished.

Exhaust Fans in End Wall

Fans at last divider (Figure 4) are the most widely recognized strategy for constrained ventilation. The air enters through the mechanized shade (winter) and is gotten through the greenhouse by the Exhaust fans.

The Exhaust fans ought to have the option to move little air volumes without drafts (winter) but give enough fan ability to an air trade inside the house every moment during summer. One air trade for each moment (without evaporative cooling) should keep the temperature around 8 degrees F higher than outside temperatures. One-portion of this air volume will deliver around a 15-degree F temperature rise, while two air trades for every moment will cause a temperature ascent of around 5 degrees F. In a perfect world, the length of the house ought not to surpass 125 feet utilizing this technique. Houses up to 250 feet in length, be that as it may, have been sufficiently ventilated utilizing this technique. Temperature varieties are more noteworthy in longer houses, so higher ventilation rates are alluring. No air must be permitted to go into the house along the frames or at the fan end.

Coating in glass houses must be very much set and the houses in decent shape to forestall critical amounts of air spilling into the house. If those cooling cushions are utilized during summer, disengage the mechanized screen and close it to keep sight-seeing from entering through the shade and bypassing the cooling cushions. You can interface a punctured plastic cylinder to a similar gulf shade to give great air conveyance to chilly climate ventilation.

A similar rule applies for numerous frame houses, gave each end divider is so prepared. One two-speed fan is generally utilized in little interest houses.

The all-out channel opening at last divider for summer ventilation (screen and evaporative cushion vent) ought to give about 1.5 square feet per 1,000 cubic feet for every moment of air travelling through the working fans. The mechanized screen and a couple of fans may be associated on one indoor regulator while the rest of the fans are associated with an alternate indoor regulator, with air being provided to these fans through the vent board containing the evaporative cushion.

Pressure Fans in End Walls

Ventilation for greenhouses that are 100 feet or shorter can be practised by mounting pressure fans, which blow air into the house, high at last dividers.

The fans at last divider are generally two-speed and constrained by independent indoor regulators. To maintain a strategic distance from high-speed air striking plants, a bewilder is set before the fans to coordinate the air toward the path wanted. The fans should have a defensive hood to keep downpour from being blown into the house.

One pressurized system where evaporative cooling is conceivable. This system puts the Pressure fans in the side divider. The pressurized system with fans in the side divider doesn't function admirably when the foliage is thick, and bunches of tall, developing plants are available. Notice the air outlet and gulf are on a similar side of the house right now, a crate fenced in area around the fan where cooling cushions are introduced.

Evaporative Cooling

The heat retained on a dull surface opposite to the sun's beams can be as high as 300 BTU/HR per square foot of surface. So it would be conceivable, hypothetically, for a greenhouse to assimilate 300 BTUs for each hour for each square foot of floor zone. This unnecessary vitality prompts heat development and, on heat days, can make plants shrivel.

Over the top heat, development can regularly be forestalled with concealing materials, for example, move up screens of wood, aluminium or vinyl plastic just as paint-on materials (concealing mixes). Move up displays, which function admirably in leisure activity houses, are available with pulleys and spoil safe nylon ropes. This screen can be balanced from outside as temperature shifts. Radiation can be diminished by 50 per cent with this technique, which ought to lessen temperature rise relatively if ventilation rate stays consistent. Concealing additionally reduces light striking the plants, which may restrict their development rate since light is basic to photosynthesis. This is an exchange of that is some of the time important to decrease temperatures.

If that late spring temperatures surpass those thoughts about satisfactory and can't be redressed with sensible ventilation rates and concealing, the main option is evaporative cooling. A fan and cushion system utilizing evaporative cooling wipes out abundance heat and includes stickiness. This decreases plant dampness misfortunes and, along these lines, lessens plant shrivelling. Temperature is brought down, moistness is expanded, and watering needs are diminished.

An evaporative cooling system moves air through a screen or shower of water in such a way, that dissipation of water happens. Around 1,000 BTUs of heat are required to change 1 pound of water from fluid to fume. If that the heat for dissipation originates from the air, the air is cooled. Vanishing is more noteworthy when the air entering the system is dry; that is, the point at which the relative stickiness is low, permitting the air to dissipate a ton of water. The water holding capacity of air is communicated as far as relative stickiness. An overall stickiness of 50 per cent, for instance, implies the air is holding one-portion of the most extreme water that the air could hold whenever immersed at a given temperature.

Hypothetically air can be cooled evaporatively until it arrives at 100 per cent relative mugginess. For all intents and purposes, a great evaporative cooler can reach around 85 per cent of this temperature drop. The cooling impact for 85 per cent productive evaporative coolers appears in Table 4.

Evaporative coolers are progressively powerful when the moistness is low (Table 4). Luckily, relative humidities are typically low during the hottest times of the day. Sun based heat going into the house counterbalances a portion of the cooling impact. An all-around designd ventilation system ace viding one air volume change for every moment is fundamental for a decent evaporative cooling system. A sun based heat increase of 8-10 degrees F can be normal, utilizing one air change for each moment. If that the outside air were 90 degrees F and relative moistness were 70 per cent, the subsequent temperature inside the house would be around 93 degrees F (83 degrees F from Table 4 in addition to 10 degrees F).

Table 4. Cooling Capacity of 85 Percent Efficient Evaporative Coolers

Outside Air   Relative Humidity

at 30% at 50% at 70% at 90%

Outside Air Temperature ºF   Cooled Air Temperature ºF

Outside Air Temperature ºF	at 30%	at 50%	at 70%	at 90%
100	79	86	91	96
90	70	77	83	87
80	63	69	74	77
70	54	60	64	68

In the event that cooling effectiveness of 85 per cent is to be acknowlframed, at any rate, 1 square foot of cushion region (aspen fibre) mounted vertically ought to be accommodated each 150 CFM of air flowed by the fans. Many cushion materials have been utilized effectively, gave a total water film doesn't frame and square air development through the wet cushion. Table 5 gives a prescribed wind current through different cushion type materials.

Table 5. Prescribed Airflow Rate through Various Pad Materials.

Cushion Type   Airflow Rate

through Pad (CFM/ft2)

Cushion Type	Airflow Rate through Pad (CFM/ft2)
Aspen fibre mounted vertically (2-4 in. thick)	150
Aspen fibre mounted evenly (2-4 in. thick)	200
Creased cellulose (4 in. thick)	250
Creased cellulose (6 in. thick)	350

Aspen cushions are usually limited in a welded wirework. A channel with firmly separated gaps permits water to run down a sheet metal spreader onto the cushions (Figure 7). The streaming pace of the water providing header pipe is recorded in Table 6. Water than doesn't dissipate noticeable all around the stream is trapped in the drain and came back to a repository for reuse. The store ought to have the ability to hold the water coming back from the cushion when the system is killed. Table 6 shows the suggested store limit with regards to various kind cushions.

Table 6. Prescribed Water Flow Rate and Reservoir Capacity for Vertically Mounted Cooling Pad Materials.

Cushion Type	Min. Flowrate per Length of Pad (GPM/ft)	Min. Repository Capacity per Unit Pad Area (Gal/ft2)
Aspen fiber (2-4 inches)	0.3	0.5
Creased cellulose (4 inches)	0.5	0.8
Creased cellulose (6 inches)	0.8	1.0

A front or some likeness thereof is expected to forestall wind stream through the cushions during the chilly climate. These can be physically worked or mechanized. Buoy control effectively controls the water supply. It is alluring to utilize an algaecide in the coursing water to forestall green growth development on the cushions. You should, subsequently, forestall downpour water from entering the evaporative cooling water, causing weakening of the substance blend.

Evaporative cushions in an endome on the suction side of fans that release air into houses (pressure fans) have not functioned admirably, essentially because of the dissemination of the cooled air. The equivalent is valid for bundle unit evaporative coolers where poor air dissemination is concerned. These units can deal with air volumes of 2,000 to 20,000 CFM. The issue with them is the trouble giving uniform cooled air appropriation. The closer the units are separated along with the dividers, the better the air circulation will be. Bundle coolers have been utilized in little houses, and in houses with great air dissemination, with significant achievement. The pressurized system powers air, which must dislodge air inside the house, into the greenhouse. Vents must be accommodated air course.

Mist Cooling

Evaporative cooling by splashing small water beads into the greenhouse has met with restricted achievement. The beads must be little, and this requires minor, firmly dispersed spouts worked at moderately high Pressures — a costly plan. Water must be very much separated to keep spouts from stopping up. Uniform appropriation of the water beads all through the house is hard to achieve.

If that the Mist system conveys any minerals in the water, stores will be left on plant foliage. This collection can diminish photosynthesis significantly and can prompt salt poisonous quality.

The Mist system can likewise cause wet foliage, prompting sickness issues, especially when the bead size is excessively huge.

Mist cooling doesn't cool as viably as a regular evaporative cooling cushion system, yet it is more affordable. The system requires no assortment skillet or sump. It can cause spillover or puddling underneath the cushions if all the water showered on the cushions isn't disintegrated.

This is in some cases called a "hazing cushion" system. A few producers have utilized it with progress.

The system ought to give roughly 20 gallons of water for each moment to be splashed on the cushion (ordinarily 20, 1-GPM shower spouts) for each 48-inch fan in the ventilation system. This measure of water, in any case, won't generally be required.

Hotter air will dissipate water quicker than cooler air. The measure of water added to the cushions can be balanced utilizing a blend of valves, time timekeepers and indoor regulators. As the temperature in the greenhouse increments, so does the recurrence of Mist spout activity.

Characteristic Ventilation

A few greenhouses can be ventilated utilizing side and frame vents, which run the full length of the house and can be opened varying to give the ideal temperature. This technique utilizes heat hillsides, making course because of heat air rising.

Houses with just side vents rely on wind pressure for ventilation and are typically not agreeable. The heat air must be permitted to ascend through the frame vent while cooler air enters at the frames. The vent size is significant. Frame vents ought to be around one-fourth the floor territory and the side vents about a similar size. The rooftop vents should open over the even situation to give around a 60-degree frame to the rooftop. The vast majority of these vents are physically worked.

Chapter Four: Lighting And Irrigation Systems

Water and light are basic to plants, and in a greenhouse, you'll need to give both. There are a few diverse watering strategies to browse: hand watering, hair-like mats that bring water up from beneath, overhead watering, and trickle water system that conveys water legitimately into each pot.

Greenhouse master Scott Naegeli says a dribble water system framework is anything but difficult to spread out and is very financially savvy. It conveys limited quantities of water over significant stretches of time, so plants remain consistently wet. The establishment is genuinely basic:

Be certain the mainline that conveys water into the greenhouse is sunk underground, in any event, four feet, which is underneath the ice line, to ensure the water in the line doesn't freeze.

Utilize a 3/4-inch poly pipe as the water supply line. It should be placed to run down the length of the seat.

From the primary line, associate horizontal lines to run between pots.

Set the framework on a clock to guarantee Regular watering.

When the water framework is set up, you'll have to address any lighting needs. Albeit bright lights are well known, they help the plant specialist more than the plants. This kind of lighting is acceptable to work by; however, plants need all the more light, particularly in northern areas.

A high-pressure sodium bulb makes a superior showing of recreating daylight to animate plant development. A 125-watt bulb radiates a lot of light when hung in any event three feet above plants or seeds. This is a decent separation to stay away from heat consume.

Develop lights help to help obscure spots and engendering zones in the greenhouse. What you are developing or causing decides to what extent you have to leave the lights on, typically a normal of 12 to 16 hours every day. If you are growing tropical plants, you may need to set up develop lights if the plants don't get in any event eight hours of sun every day.

Chapter Five: Planning For A Greenhouse Seeds

While numerous seeds can be planted legitimately in the greenhouse in fall or spring and really develop best from common climate changes, different seeds are significantly more finicky and require consistent temperatures and a controlled situation to sprout. By beginning seeds in a greenhouse, cultivators can give a steady climate to seeds to grow and seedlings to develop. Keep perusing to figure out how to plant seeds in a greenhouse. When to Plant Greenhouse Seeds Greenhouses permit you to control the temperature and stickiness required for seed proliferation and young seedlings to develop. In view of this controlled condition, you can really begin seeds in greenhouses whenever. If you are beginning plants, which you intend to transplant into greenhouses outside in the spring, at that point, you should start the seeds in greenhouses 6 two months before the last expected ice date for your area. For best achievement, most seeds ought to be developed in temperatures around 70-80 F. (21-27 C.), with night temperatures that don't plunge lower than 50-55 F. (10-13 C.). The temperature in your greenhouse ought to be deliberately checked. Greenhouses are commonly heat during the day when the sun is sparkling, yet can get a lot cooler around evening time. Seedling heat mats can help give seeds reliably heat soil temperatures. Greenhouses that are furnished with fans or opening windows can vent greenhouses that have gotten excessively hot.

Greenhouse Seed Starting

Seeds are generally originated in greenhouses in open level seed plate or individual attachment plate. Seeds are prepared by their particular needs; for instance, they might be doused medium-term, scarified or stratified, at that point planted in the plate the greenhouse.

In open level plate, seeds are usually planted in pleasantly divided columns for simplicity of diminishing, watering, preparing and treating seedling maladies, for example, damping off. At that point, when these seedlings produce their first arrangement of genuine leaves, they are transplanted into singular pots or cells. In single-cell plate, just a couple of seeds is planted per cell. Numerous specialists feel that planting in plug plate is superior to open plate on the grounds that the attachment cells hold and hold more dampness and heatth for the creating seed. Seedlings can likewise remain in plug plate longer without their foundations turning out to be entwined with their neighbours. Seedlings in fittings can just be jumped out and transplanted directly into the greenhouse or holder courses of action. When beginning seeds in a greenhouse, you don't have to spend a fortune on extraordinary seed beginning blends. You can blend your own universally useful preparing blend by including 1 equivalent part peat greenery, 1 section perlite and 1 section natural material, (for example, fertilizer). It is, in any case, very important that any preparing medium you use be disinfected between utilizations to slaughter off pathogens that can prompt the seedling illness known as damping off. Additionally, if temperatures are excessively cool in the greenhouse, light isn't sufficiently severe, or if seedlings are overwatered, they may create leggy, powerless stems.

Chapter Five: Greenhouse Environment

Your crop creation can turn out to be exceptionally quickened using greenhouse condition control framework or mechanization. With this type of environmental control, the greenhouse remains consistent to give ideal conditions that are generally ideal for most extreme crop.

A plant's capacity to develop and create is needy predominantly on Photosynthesis. Within sight of light, the plant joins carbon dioxide and water to frame sugars which are then used for development and bloom/natural product creation.

The executives of the greenhouse condition are aimed at enhancing the photosynthetic procedure in the plants, the plant's capacity to use light at most extreme proficiency.

Greenhouse Lighting Control

There's much more to Greenhouse lighting than meets the eye. Producers looking for the fitting light for their Greenhouse ought to think about the accompanying three factors: the sort of harvest being developed, what season it is, and how a lot of daylight is available.

Greenhouses, by and large, require six hours of direct or full-range light every day. On the off chance that this isn't possible usually, supplemental lighting must be fused. Additional lighting is the utilization of numerous, high-force fake lights to advance harvest development and crop. Specialists like to utilize them to keep up growth and expand the developing season, though business cultivators use them to support returns and benefits.

Producers have a full cluster of lighting alternatives to pick from, so it's imperative to comprehend the subtleties of varying lighting styles. Again this gets simpler to make do with Greenhouse environmental controls that can be planned and checked.

Stickiness Control

As plants increment their pace of development, you'll need to bring down stickiness gradually to support transpiration, which permits more water to move through the plant. As the plant devours more water, the top of the prolonged cell and bring supplements off to the developing pieces of the plant.

Moistness ought to likewise be observed cautiously provided that gets excessively high in Greenhouses; plant leaves stand a greatly improved possibility of getting wet. Wet leaves, tragically, is perhaps the ideal approaches to guarantee contagious contamination or an episode of buildup. Parasitic illnesses, for example, the Botrytis pathogen or fine mold are basic greenhouse offenders. To screen and control the Greenhouse condition implies better quality control.

Ventilation and Fan Control

Another simple method to help direct temperature and moistness is the utilization of vents. With the use of rack and pinons and ventilation control, you can trigger the Greenhouse vents to open at a set temperature on the off chance that it begins to find a good pace.

Likewise, we are estimating the relative dampness (the measure of water fume present in air communicated as a level of the sum required for immersion.) which can likewise be brought down by opening the vents—heat dry air and not wet.

We can likewise trigger level wind stream fans with Greenhouse control frameworks. These improve the dissemination of air and help to oust stickiness out of the air. It is essential to build the Greenhouse temperatures for an appropriate parity.

With the utilization of appropriate Greenhouse temperature and mugginess sensors, this is completely controlled through our Greenhouse robotization PC. This will assist you with monitoring and direct mugginess and temp levels all the more viably. Our producer endorsed Greenhouse natural control programming guarantees all levels remain under tight restraints.

Carbon Dioxide or Co2 Control

Conveying a lot of carbon dioxide to your plants is fundamental for substantial plant development. Plants accept carbon from the air, just like a significant segment of photosynthesis. Carbon dioxide goes into the plant through the stomatal openings by the procedure of dissemination.

CO2 builds efficiency through improved plant development and by and large wellbeing. A few manners by which efficiency is expanded by CO2 incorporate before blossoming, higher organic product crops and longer development cycles.

Getting into a portion of the more specialized math here, however, for most of Greenhouse crops, net photosynthesis increments as CO2 levels increment from 340–1,000 ppm (parts per million).

Most crops show that for some random degree of photosynthetically active radiation (PAR), expanding the CO2 level to 1,000 ppm will build the photosynthesis by about half over encompassing CO2 levels.

Remain in quality control rules with our Greenhouse atmosphere control framework to appropriately control CO2 ranges.

Air Temperature Control

Expanding air temperature will build the pace of photosynthesis to a point. Nonetheless, over 85 degrees, plants go into photorespiration. Which isn't ideal for developing, plants will begin to shrivel.

Also, if you don't coordinate the higher air temperatures with more significant levels of carbon dioxide and light force, your plants will accomplish more photorespiration than photosynthesis, which will negatively affect your plants' wellbeing.

At one point, proteins won't play out their capacities and will self-destruct, and your plants won't set up sound digestion. In everything, balance is vital, with our Greenhouse temperature control framework.

Regular Irrigation and Fertilizers – Fertigation Control

We like to a Regular water system and supplement feed equation for crops in the Greenhouse. In the present enormous business tasks, this is the place fertigation mechanization can assist, however, assist you with excursion perform on every other ranch.

Fertigation continually applies water and composts at exact sums through the water system framework. This providing of supplements required by the harvests helps keep crops at their best.

Fertigation is particularly helpful on account of a trickle water system. With our computerized fertigation hardware, the water and the supplements are ingested straightforwardly into the roots improving the pace of development, versatility and nature of the crops.

This framework is progressively judicious utilization of water and composts. I think regarding nature and limiting the ecological effect is something we would all be able to get behind. We can likewise utilize a Greenhouse water reusing framework to guarantee your crops security.

Complete Greenhouse Automation

Mechanization can assume a tremendous job in your Greenhouse condition and making quality indoor becoming suitable. At Climate Control Systems Inc, we have been helping cultivators remain productive for more than 35 years.

Our control innovation empowers cultivators to program their own developing condition how they'd like. Any adjustments in developing conditions can be immediately revised through computerization. With our progressed IIOT guaranteed frameworks producers can screen their indoor developing condition from their cell phones or PCs.

This innovation has been at the foundation of beneficial producers who need to bring down vitality, work and compost costs. This also, boosting crop crops and the arrival on speculation for new developing innovation.

Chapter Six: Essential Greenhouse Equipment

Having great greenhouse equipment and greenhouse extras can be crucial to dealing with a greenhouse proficiently.

So as to have the option to deliver great, all year crops, you should realize what sort of greenhouse equipment to purchase.

As indoor developing is turning into a standard practice for producers around the world, your greenhouse equipment and frill should fit into very close spaces and smaller than regular greenhouses.

We should see what the best greenhouse equipment and supplies required when beginning greenhouse cultivating are:

Best Greenhouse equipment you need

One of the fundamental highlights of a productive greenhouse configuration is having the correct accomplices to encourage developing harvests.

More on top hacks for a greenhouse plan in this article.

Types of greenhouse equipment

1. Rudiments

2. Greenhouse furniture

3. Water the board — Irrigation and seepage

4. Lighting

5. Atmosphere control and heating

6. Ventilation

7. Irritation control

Every last one of these segments should be made arrangements for while developing greenhouses.

As you read on, we'll examine the different things that come in every classification.

Fundamental greenhouse equipment

What strikes a chord when you consider starting your planting pastime?

Perhaps not a whole greenhouse, however certainly seeds, pots and plate?

These are the essential things you have to begin developing plants.

Your decision of greenhouse compartments is urgent in light of the fact that it will largely affect how your vegetables or plants develop.

For a greenhouse holder, planters can utilize whatever grasps soil as long as it meets these meets two criteria:

Right off the bat, it ought to advance great wellbeing, giving a lot of room for roots and giving superb seepage.

Also, it should hold the harvest well and settle its upward development.

There are numerous assortments of compartments like pads and fittings, hanging crates and pots.

There are much bigger compartments that are prepared to hold different little pots.

Hanging crates are ideal for developing plants, blossoms and vegetables in stature while utilizing space.

They can be produced using plastic, metal artistic or even coconut fiber.

Attachments and level holders are utilized every now and again for early germination purposes.

These compartments are available to hold different little plants or blossoms while keeping them isolated.

With respect to preparing, greenhouse workers incline toward greenhouse pots produced using earth since they are the conventional method for developing the blossoms and plants.

Nonetheless, if that you can't purchase earth pots, you can consider materials like plastic, wood, peat greenery and wood fiber too.

These are frequently lighter in weight, more strong and less expensive than dirt pots.

They are effectively expendable too.

Seedboxes are additionally viewed as basic greenhouse equipment.

Plastic seedboxes are taking over from the wood encloses that numerous cultivators utilized the past.

The advantages and disadvantages of plastic versus wood are as yet being bantered far and wide.

If that you truly need to practice environmental safety, cut the plastic alternative and remain with wood.

In any case, get seedboxes that are around 14 inches X 8 inches X 2 inches.

This is the ideal size to develop infant seeds.

Another extremely decent plan contact are Rain Chains like these copper downpour chains.

Picking great greenhouse pots and compartments:

The soil in permeable greenhouse compartments can dry out soon, and you'll need to water it on different occasions, thus squandering water.

In non-permeable compartments, the dirt will in general hold dampness better, in this way turning away over-watering.

At the point when you're picking greenhouse pots and compartments, remember that they ought to accomplish more than fulfil a plant's development needs; they ought to likewise have enormous waste and porosity.

By and large, in case you're anticipating all year crops, you'll have to get ready for versatility.

Your greenhouse pots should be effectively mobile and lightweight.

You'll be sure that your compartments are eco-accommodating, which will, thusly, take into account the ideal conceivable condition for your plant.

Right greenhouse pots and supplies can raise infant plants from seeds in any event when the dirt isn't good for germination.

Picking the correct kind of greenhouse compartment will have an enormous effect on the general improvement of your greenhouse plants.

Furniture to store your greenhouse equipment and plants

Very much arranged furnishings and satisfactory racking inside a greenhouse are basic to store every one of your pots and compartments.

In a little greenhouse design with restricted space, racking can support the developing zone with no adverse effects on conceal.

Some greenhouse racks are portable (with haggles) be moved outside during perfect climate and afterwards back inside around evening time or during cold temperatures.

Racks might be made from materials, for example, glass, wood or metal.

It is critical to recall that if twofold racking is utilized, the measure of lighting arriving at plants might be influenced.

To spare space, you can likewise find retires underneath greenhouse seats.

Greenhouse racks can be brief for beginning seedlings or lasting, connected to the greenhouse design.

Soot, wood squares and metal are perfect for the legs and stands of the racks.

The wire lattices of the racks empower abundance water to deplete off.

Greenhouse racking can likewise help keep crops isolated to forestall seeding or cross-fertilization.

Greenhouse seats are one type of racking that takes into consideration most extreme space and capacity.

Their optimal size is commonly dictated by the width of the greenhouse so as to improve developing space.

Seats might be lasting apparatuses or impermanent ones.

If that you mean to consistently evacuate or adjust them, at that point separated seat choices might be beneficial for you.

Read in insight regarding greenhouse seats and their numerous utilizations in our blog article here.

The grower is another kind of greenhouse furniture that is generally utilized in the present planting field.

Long and profound grower are typically prescribed for nourishment crops.

These can be produced using different materials like plastic, wood or metal.

They are commonly organized such that every grower contains just a single vegetable.

Greenhouse Irrigation and seepage Equipment

You'll require approaches to water your plants over the span of their lives.

While programmed watering frameworks are viral, there will consistently be a unique spot in Regular planting for past watering jars.

The long gushes on the jars will effectively arrive at all of your plants even at the rear of the blossom bed.

Greenhouse Water the board

You'll likewise have the option to alter your watering experience dependent on what every individual bed needs.

In the watering can portion as well, plastic is assuming control over metal.

Plastic jars are commonly lighter, which makes watering less work concentrated.

In addition, they are regularly less expensive.

Be that as it may, if that greenhouse feel is your thing, at that point stay with the metal jars.

Another kind of greenhouse equipment is the stream watering framework.

Best Retractable Greenhouse Hose Reels

Greenhouse Trickle Watering System

Make a stream watering framework with a plastic hose that has outlet spouts at various interims all through its length.

Set the hose along with your pots at a fitting closeness.

Associate your hose to a capacity tank that fills reliably and discharges water at whatever point it is full.

What's extraordinary about this framework is it will water your pots or beds in the specific amounts you want, at the particular time each day!

Different types of water the executives greenhouse equipment you will require are acceptable cylinders, water breakers, valves, sirs, hoses, sprinklers and boilers for directing temperatures.

Recollect that you should discover a place in your greenhouse or yard to store these things.

Greenhouse Lighting

The lighting framework inside a greenhouse decides the degree of daylight, artificial light and shade for the plants.

You may need to consider artificial lighting if the daylight in your general vicinity isn't sufficient.

To encourage sufficient lighting, you may need to purchase:

- Develop lights
- Seedling lights
- LEDs
- General universally handy lighting
- High-power lights

While having a broad lighting framework might be costly for little greenhouses, for bigger ones, it is practically required.

Allude to our all-around investigated and itemized article on picking the best greenhouse lights here.

Atmosphere control and heating greenhouse equipment

These are frequently stout types of greenhouse equipment intended to control the measure of mugginess, heatth and ice inside the greenhouse.

We should take a gander at the principal parts of an atmosphere control framework:

Greenhouse thermometers

The way into a productive greenhouse is in keeping up ideal temperature consistently, which makes a thermometer significant.

Introduce a thermometer that registers most extreme and least temperatures with a needle position that shows up when the mercury withdraws.

With regards to thermometers for greenhouses, you'll need one that can be reset with a magnet.

There are all the more excellent quality choices that have press button rearrangements, yet they are redundant.

Thermometers are required for a wide range of greenhouses, even convenient ones.

Likewise, consider a dirt thermometer to check the temperature of the dirt.

Greenhouse indoor regulator

A greenhouse indoor regulator empowers you to know the overarching temperature in your greenhouse and direct it in like manner.

A temperature measure or thermometer shows the temperature changes while an indoor regulator consequently controls the temperature in the ideal zone.

In a perfect world, a great greenhouse ought to have an indoor regulator.

Greenhouse heaters

Other significant greenhouse equipment manages to deal with the heatth inside the greenhouse.

Greenhouse heaters are essential to control the temperature in a greenhouse.

They come in different materials, with various modes and vitality sources.

You can choose from electric, gas and propane radiators as indicated by your necessities and prerequisites.

You likewise have the alternative of either choosing a vented or non-vented radiator.

Greenhouse humidistat

Greenhouse humidifiers or humidistat are essential to control the measure of dampness in the greenhouse.

A few plants are defenceless to dry air, which will hamper their vegetative development.

This issue without much of a stretch is fathomed with the assistance of a viable humidistat.

Ventilation equipment for your greenhouse

Legitimate ventilation is obligatory for appropriate plant development, during specific seasons, yet lasting through the year.

This is on the grounds that, whenever of the year, the sun is fit for causing extraordinary movements of temperature.

A decent guideline is to have open venting alternatives equivalent to about 20% of the floor zone.

Vents might be situated on the rooftop and sides of the design, just as included as a feature of the entryway.

Rooftop venting is esteemed as the most perfectly awesome when coming to fixing vent frameworks.

Numerous programmed venting frameworks are perfect alternatives for the individuals who are not around to deal with the greenhouse all for the duration of the day.

Fumes fans are another likelihood for venting overabundance air; however, whether they are a shrewd decision for any circumstance, specifically, merits explore.

Nuisance control equipment

No rundown of greenhouse equipment would be finished without things for bother control.

There are different strategies for viable nuisance control; some that utilization synthetic substances and others that utilization science.

Synthetic concoctions are anything but difficult to utilize and genuinely cheap, yet some would contend that they accomplish more damage than anything else.

Typical techniques, for example, utilizing what is usually called "advantageous creepy crawlies" are another type of battling bugs.

These bugs basically chase down and eat the bugs that ruin your greenhouse.

In some cases, all the plant needs is a decent work to keep bugs outside.

Such networks can be of metal, fabric or slight plastic.

You may likewise require fencing and entryway breadths to keep bugs out of explicit zones.

There are various types of misting equipment, foamers and sprayers that target bugs.

Bug sprays and pesticides ought to be utilized sparingly, with the primary inclination going to natural or normal splashes to keep bothers from assaulting crops.

Greenhouse equipment and embellishments

Soil sterilizers

Whatever dirt you are thinking about utilizing for preparing your plants, it would be unbelievably valuable to have a dirt sterilizer.

There are numerous approaches to clean soil; however, the best and most productive one is by introducing a steam cleansing framework.

Steam frameworks are helpful and suitable.

They won't occupy especially space and work superbly on your dirt.

Planting Sieve – Sowing Sieve

The surface of the dirt is a significant component to consider when planting your little child plants.

A planting sifter will be useful in helping you accomplish your ideal surface.

A work sifter can be utilized to gently cover your seeds with manure after you've planted them.

The uplifting news is you don't really need to purchase a sifter.

This bit of greenhouse equipment can be a DIY venture.

Utilize a little wooden box like the ones you purchase mass organic products.

Take out the base of the case and spot a bit of punctured zinc in there, and presto — you have your own one of a kind strainer!

You can designate this straightforward action to your children and family as well.

Plant bolster equipment

To guarantee your plants develop in quality and length, you'll have to offer satisfactory help for them.

Here and there, you should simply integrate up the plants, so they bolster one another.

While there are numerous materials utilized for tying your plants, we propose raffia as it is sensibly estimated and can bolster most plants.

HACK: Soak the raffia in water for a couple of hours before utilizing it. This makes it flexible, and it won't split or break when tying solid bunches.

You will likewise be protected with fillis, a delicate twine that comes in numerous kinds.

Split rings, green cultivating twine and paper-secured wires are likewise utilized by numerous greenhouse producers.

You can likewise utilize fencing and greenhouse molds to shape plants into wanted designs.

Where to purchase greenhouse embellishments and supplies

Numerous people are presently taking up greenhouse planting as an interest.

As they attempt to accomplish their planting objectives, they have to improve their aptitudes by getting fundamental cultivating adornments and supplies.

In any case, loads of cultivating supplies can be costly.

Purchasing from places that sell discount greenhouse supplies can bring down expenses.

You can likewise get limited greenhouse extras and supplies a slow time of year.

There are a lot of approaches to find limited greenhouse supplies and providers.

Purchasing greenhouse equipment and extras from wholesalers versus retailers

Many discount greenhouse supplies can be found through nearby providers and ranch associations.

Since heaps of large organizations purchase their things in mass, these items regularly have the ideal arrangements on greenhouse cultivating supplies.

Likewise, the vast majority of these organizations utilize people who are specialists right now.

This can end up being a dependable asset for a novice planter.

Large greenhouse planting chains regularly sell discount supplies.

Once more, since they regularly purchase in mass, they are prepared to offer excellent arrangements.

They likewise, for the most part, have yearly greenhouse embellishments deals that can additionally support your reserve funds.

The costs of providers or wholesalers are less expensive, contrasted with retail prices.

Additionally, buying discount greenhouse frill from wholesalers gives you better quality items with a more extensive scope of determinations available.

Subsequently, you can find different greenhouse providers in neighbourhood registries and other online destinations committed to discount things.

The absolute most basic greenhouse frill offered in discount rates are greenery, snares, liners, sections and iron casing holders.

There are additionally various different things sold in mass like plant markers, composts, bolsters, watering jars and dampness maintenance things.

Other typical greenhouse extras incorporate manure pails, plant stands, sharpeners, pruners, pot feet and enhancing supplies.

You will likewise need to discover places that sell gloves, soil and scoops for your cultivating interests.

Greenhouse Equipment

Discount Greenhouse Supplies at Orchid Greenhouse

Becoming environmentally viable with greenhouse units

Having a greenhouse and developing plants can be a genuine delight for the spirit.

Incredible watering frameworks, sterile soil and extraordinary beds are only a couple of things you'll need for an ideal greenhouse.

When settling on your equipment by choices, consider the accompanying with the goal that your decisions can be in a more fabulous condition well disposed.

Naturally Friendly Greenhouses

Think about utilizing biodegradable pots. Reuse existing pots and old furniture as greenhouse equipment and supplies.

Check your current supplies to check whether they are confirmed and institutionalized.

Utilize characteristic composts and vermin control techniques over synthetic concoctions.

Utilizing jute, fabric and woollen strings to hold up plants or give conceal sets aside cash and pointless acquisition of hurtful plastic or pitch.

Introduce a water framework that gathers overabundance run-off and re-consolidates it into the water table.

Spare time, vitality and fuel spent on numerous outings by buying a single greenhouse unit that will give all of you have to make a greenhouse without any preparation in a little bundle.

You can likewise consider leasing the greenhouse supplies you can't stand to purchase in the event that you possess smaller than usual or medium-sized greenhouses.

For more tips on keeping greenhouses green, you can generally look at our Greenhouse Learning Center.

Greenhouses and their embellishments:

Best Greenhouse Accessories

Developing plants in greenhouses has become a manageable and productive diversion for some right now.

To develop great practical nourishment, it's fundamental to claim a steady greenhouse and appropriate equipment to run consistently.

Greenhouse equipment ought to be eco-accommodating and financially savvy to support the proprietor and the earth.

There are a few kinds of greenhouse equipment, extensively partitioned into preparing, furniture, atmosphere control and water system frameworks, composts, bug control and smaller than expected extras like gloves, scoops and instruments.

Fumes fans, bloom bins, sprinkler frameworks, indoor regulators, radiators and shade materials are a portion of the basic things expected to run a medium-to-huge size greenhouse.

When buying these things, you will require satisfactory racking and capacity territories to keep them protected and secure.

Use home things as greenhouse seats and kitchen holders as pots are acceptable approaches to get a good deal on equipment.

Else, you can discover discount vendors who sell seed plate, covers, channels and instruments in mass.

You can likewise lease greenhouse equipment to spare expense and time.

Chapter Seven: Using Space Effectively

The most effective method to Maximize Your Space

Regardless of whether you as of now have a little greenhouse in your lawn or you are considering buying one, these space-sparing tips will assist you with maximizing your space in a little greenhouse. A great many people, who live in urban regions don't have a ton of room and need to make the most out of their patio. Others simply need more cash to put resources into an enormous greenhouse or simply start with greenhouse planting as a diversion. In spite of the fact that we generally prescribe getting one size bigger than you might suspect, we comprehend that there are conditions that make it outlandish. In this manner, we need to give you thoughts on the best way to benefit as much as possible from your little greenhouse.

What is a little greenhouse?

Consider anything up to 65 square feet as little. In the event that you haven't bought your greenhouse yet, we have an incredible assortment for you to read here.

6 Space-sparing tips for amplifying your space

1. Surface region

Figure the whole surface zone available in your greenhouse to check whether you are utilizing the area open to you. With little greenhouse units, individually, each and every piece of room tallies. In this way, you ought to guarantee that you boost the all-out surface territory in your greenhouse.

One approach to do this is to utilize moving seats or to get a little greenhouse unit, for example, the Solexx 8ft x 8ft Greenhouse Master or the onion-formed Riga 2s that have pre-worked in racking. These packs, for the most part, boost the developing space productively.

2. Crop designs and arranging

Where conceivable, attempt to utilize your greenhouse at close full limit. Consider what season you are in and begin developing plants that can withstand colder temperatures early. Make an arrangement of the plants that you need to build. At that point plan everything from planting to gathering with the goal that you can utilize the greenhouse space to the maximum capacity. A few plants take shorter occasions to be prepared for gathering, for instance, spinach and radishes. When you reaped those, you can utilize the spot for developing something different or the equivalent, it's up to you, obviously.

You can likewise plan your harvests to transplant them into your greenhouse.

3. Transplanting plants

Contingent upon the season you can begin your plants inside your little greenhouse and transplant them into your greenhouse. This spares space inside your greenhouse as well as gives you an extraordinary head start the outside developing season.

Utilize these seed plate for rearranging this undertaking!

Transplants can be increasingly insusceptible to bug and different irritations since they are progressively evolved and more significant when you previously put them into your greenhouse. There is no problem with flying creatures picking your seeds in your greenhouse beds outside.

Incredible instances of vegetables that can be transplanted in the wake of developing them in seed plate:

- Celery
- Eggplant
- Collards
- Kale
- Broccoli
- Kohlrabi
- Leeks
- Onion
- Peppers
- Scallions
- Tomato

4. Greenhouse layering and arranging

Could crops be layered? On occasion, including a second harvest under your first planting will work splendidly until the plants grow. For instance, utilizing cress over yields that take more time to develop.

Greenhouse arranging is famous for cultivators. It gives a lot of surface zone for your seedlings and plants. It boosts the developing vertical space, as well. By arranging your harvests, you make increasingly concealed regions underneath the seats. This can be gainful for those species that develop consummately under low light conditions. Kale and other verdant vegetables simply work fine in obscure spaces (discover more plants for unknown places here).

Get all the more arranging and racking thoughts here!

In any case, different plants need more daylight, so you need to design your harvests and partition your greenhouse into zones.

5. Zoning

Separating your yard into zones will assist you with utilizing the space most productively. As referenced above, you can use for the plan. You can likewise consider setting your harvests relying upon how a lot of heatth they need. Plant the crops that just develop in heat temperatures near the heatth sources. At that point, put your cool tolerant harvests somewhat isolated from the heatth. Along these lines, you have the ideal conditions for developing your crops quicker and all the more proficiently.

Zoning your greenhouse isn't only for developing effectiveness yet in addition to the association. Picture seats and retires. Arranging various locales for your plants will lessen the messiness and will get bothers far from the greenhouse. Keep things you for the most part use in one spot, and you won't burn through important time looking for them. Arranging zoned spaces in your greenhouse is an incredible plan to guarantee you're taking advantage of the spot you have.

6. Snares, hanging pots and other greenhouse accomplices to boost the space in a little greenhouse

Vertical planting assists with using small spaces to their most extreme. Use snares, spirals, top retires or draping pots from the rooftop or side dividers. You can either utilize it for developing, for drying herbs, or for putting away cultivating apparatuses. Be imaginative. Clasp together planting gloves or seed parcels and balance them on the dividers with a snare. Hanging pots add a fascinating plan to your greenhouse whenever set in higher regions. For usability, you can utilize the Plant Caddie Hook. You can undoubtedly bring down your pots with it to make dealing with your plants more available.

Putting more retires as an afterthought divider builds the developing vertical space radically. Moreover, it looks pretty, and you can even store planting devices on the snares.

Introducing pot holders or snares is another extraordinary choice to improve the space in a little greenhouse.

Hanging pots can be a remarkable expansion to your greenhouse too! You can put them as high you need them with the goal that you despite everything have enough headroom to stroll through your greenhouse helpfully.

By deliberately arranging your little greenhouse, you can proficiently boost the space in your modest house. Utilize the tips and tricks given above to take advantage of your small greenhouse.

Chapter Eight: Growing In Your Green House

Tomatoes

Tomatoes prove to be fruitful productively and require almost no upkeep, so they are among the most mainstream vegetables for home greenhouses. Sufficient heatth and long, bright days are essential for the plants to hold up under organic product, so they are just beneficial throughout the mid-year and harvest time a long time inside U.S. Division of Agriculture plant solidness zones 8 to 10. Be that as it may, planting tomatoes inside a greenhouse will successfully expand the developing season and permit the plants to hold up under all year, if that they are furnished with the best possible light, soil and temperature conditions.

1. Plant determinate, or hframe type, tomatoes in greenhouses instead of uncertain assortments since the last become enormous and will occupy an excess of room. Pick cultivars, for example, "Legend," "Yard Hybrid" and "Cherry Grande Hybrid."

2. Plant greenhouse tomatoes in harvest time or late-winter for a late or early crop. Start the seeds inside four to about a month and a half before transplanting them into the greenhouse to guarantee they are full-grown and solidified off.

3. Set up the greenhouse before planting the tomatoes. Hang 10-percent conceal material along with the southerly mass of the greenhouse to forestall sunburn. Spot a greenhouse seat along the southerly divider. Position a thermometer close to the greenhouse seat to screen the temperature.

4. Pot the tomatoes in 5-gallon compartments loaded up with a dirt blend of 3 sections soil, 2 sections manure, 1 section coarse sand and 1 section perlite. Plant the youthful tomatoes with the goal that the base of the stem is 1/2-inch beneath the outside of the dirt to help make sturdier, increasingly hearty develop plants.

5. Spot the tomatoes on the greenhouse seat close to the thermometer. Give water at whatever point the dirt blend feels dry in the top inch. Feed the plants with low-nitrogen, 5-10-5 compost one month in the wake of planting. Apply the manure at half-quality. Feed once every month and water entirely after each sustaining.

6. Keep up a steady daytime temperature of 70 to 80 F and an evening temperature of around 65 F. Try not to permit the temperature to dip under 65 F around evening time since the organic product will turn out to be coarse and unpalatable. Try not to let the greenhouse heat up over 85 F since the natural outcome will be stained.

7. Open the ventilation course to circle the heat air and wipe out overabundance dampness, which will help forestall leaf spot and curse. Turn on a swaying fan if the temperature transcends 85 F or if relative mugginess tops 70 F.

8. Furnish supplemental light utilizing greenhouse lights with bright light bulbs. Position the lights roughly 3 feet over the tomato plants. Point the lights, so the light looks off the highest points of the plants. Turn on the lights throughout the winter months when there is under eight hours of direct daylight.

9. Watch for indications of ailments, for example, leaf spot and curse, which are exceptionally typical in greenhouse conditions. Search for slight injuries on the leaves or shrivelled foliage. Expel and wreck the distressed plants to keep the disease from spreading.

Things You Will Need

- 10-percent conceal material
- Thermometer
- 5-gallon holders
- Soil
- Fertilizer
- Coarse sand
- Perlite
- 5-10-5 proportion compost
- Greenhouse heater
- Swaying fan
- Greenhouse light with bright light bulb

Tips

- Turn the pots by a half-unrest like clockwork to give even light introduction.
- Prune off any leggy development to drive the tomato plant's vitality toward organic product creation.
- Keep up a dirt pH of around 6.5, which is somewhat acidic.
- Space the pots with the goal that the air flows openly between the plants.

Potatoes

Potatoes are a staple element for some individuals, so having the option to become your own can be valuable. It's likewise fulfilling to have the option to develop your personal delivery and can be a great deal of amusing to do, in any event, for learners. Potatoes are undeniably fit greenhouse developing, as being inside a greenhouse can help keep potatoes from being influenced by unfavourable climate conditions or ice.

In what Can You Plant Potatoes?

Probably the most ideal methods for developing potatoes, and one that works viably in a greenhouse, is to utilize an enormous holder, barrel or sack. Greenhouse focuses and DIY stores regularly sell massive holders and uncommon hard-wearing bags that you can use to plant potatoes, however a decent, and frequently less expensive, elective is to utilize a huge canister.

All things considered, if you need to plant three seed potatoes, at that point, you'll require a compartment that estimates 24 inches high and around 18 creeps in measurement. To plant five seed potatoes, your holder ought to be 30 inches tall, and 24 crawls in the distance across.

Step by step instructions to Plant Potatoes

There is a wide range of varieties of potatoes available, each trimming at marginally various occasions. At the point when you've worked out which type you'd prefer to develop, the fastest and most straightforward methodology for learners is to buy seed potatoes from a greenhouse community.

Try not to plant the seed potatoes straight away, however – first it's ideal for chitting the potatoes. Chitting is a simple procedure, whereby you urge the potatoes to begin growing before you plant them in your greenhouse. Chitting can be initiated from late January or February, with the end goal of planting around about a month and a half later, when the shoots are about 0.5 inches to 1 inch long.

Plant your chitted potatoes from mid-April. Guarantee your picked compartment has gaps for seepage at the base, with a layer of rock or broken pots, at that point include your fertilizer. Spot your seed potatoes into the pot, in any event, five inches separated, and add more fertilizer top.

When planted, attempt and position the pots of potatoes with the goal that they're in a territory of the greenhouse that will get a decent measure of sun consistently. Water usually, yet take care not to overwater them.

At the point when the first shoots start to show up, you have to cover them up with more soil. Keep on doing this as more shoots show up – your potato plants should wind up having a little hill of soil around them – as they like to develop in dull conditions and with the shoots underneath the dirt, as opposed to presented to sunlight.

Contingent upon which sort of potato you've planted, they ought to be prepared to reap from June through to September.

Cucumbers

Cucumbers are a substantially more different crop than the vast majority acknowlframe: general stores have given a great many people the feeling that the waxless English cucumber and the gherkin are the main two alternatives available; however, most plant specialists know better.

Lesser-realized determinations have different flavors and surfaces. The sweet, round, yellow Lemon cucumber is extraordinary for making cucumber water and for crisp eating. Somewhat severe, tough German Schälgurken is ideal for fricasseeing. Round Dosakai cucumbers, hailing from India, are incredible for making chutney.

Picking Your Cucumbers

Cucumbers can be a convoluted harvest to develop flawlessly, so selecting the correct cultivar for greenhouse development is urgent.

Atmosphere: Outdoor or Greenhouse?

A few cultivars of cucumber can be developed outside, so while they can be originated in the greenhouse, they are best moved out into the greenhouse once temperatures consider it. Cucumber plants occupy a ton of room, so just the ones that should be in the greenhouse for the entire season ought to stay there.

Shape: Bush or Vine?

Hframe cucumbers have short vines on which they bear their organic products, as they have been reproduced to take up a negligible measure of room. By and large, they will require around 1 m2 of room.

Vine cucumbers need a trellis or help, as they will append and develop vertically whenever given the opportunity. Then again, they can be left to develop along with the dirt; however, utilizing vertical space provides a much much-improved on of constrained greenhouse land.

Family: Heirloom or Hybrid?

Legacy cukes can offer some genuinely fascinating hues and flavors. Cultivars like Crystal Apple White Spine and Boothby's Blonde have one of a kind attributes that aren't really coordinated in more current mixtures.

Half breeds do, be that as it may, for the most part, have the benefit of being simpler to trim just as heavier editing, and more infection safe.

Subsequently, the decision is, for the most part, a matter of individual inclination. Why not attempt both?

Reason: Slicing, Pickling, or Burpless?

Cutting cucumbers are for crisp eating and are commonly long, smooth, natural products that are picked early, while they are still sweet.

Pickling cucumbers- - "gherkins" or "wallies" in the vernacular- - are quite obvious: they are the best determinations for long haul conservation. Most cut cucumbers can likewise be cured psyche you, however, the best picklers have been reared for consistency long and measurement, just as a reliable, without void inside the substance. They likewise never have waxed skin.

Supposed "burpless" cucumbers are developed for their dainty skin and absence of seeds, which are implied to give a few people gas. They can be utilized for either cutting or pickling.

Planting and Care

Sowing

Cucumber seeds ought to be planted around three weeks before they are to be transplanted, so ascertain as indicated by where they will be planted and temperature forecasts for the season. They grow best at a dirt temperature of between 21 to 29? C.

Transplanting

Most squash-type plants don't especially like being transplanted, so moving the plant from the cell or pot in which it sprouted to its perpetual home for the season is fitting.

Fruiting

Cucumber fertilization is marginally confused and relies vigorously upon which kind of plants have been chosen.

Parthenocarpic or seedless natural products - like "burpless" cukes- - are typically developed inside a greenhouse that avoids honey bees, so as to shield them from being pollinated.

Some cucumber plants that require fertilization, then again, have male blossoms and female blossoms that sprout at various occasions, or are "self-contradictory." They need a fertilization accomplice of another cultivar.

More current crossover cultivars produce for the most part female blossoms, which implies they bear more organic product, gave adequate fertilization.

Pests and Diseases

The best creepy-crawly dangers to cucumbers- - and most squash-type plants- - are stem borers and certain insects. Great cleanliness and careful investigation of plants can help stop issues before they start.

Eggplant

Aubergines (eggplants) are turning out to be famous vegetables to develop at home - on account of new cultivars progressively fit the British atmosphere and their scrumptious natural product. Daylight and heat growing conditions are the way to progress. A seed is planted right off the bat in the year, so a plant propagator is priceless; on the other hand, develop seedlings in the airing organizer.

Sow

Sow at 18-21°C (65-70°F) in seed-planting manure in pots or modules. In the event that sprouting seeds in the airing cabinet, check seeds day by day and evacuate them when they have developed.

For greenhouse development: utilize a heated propagator and sow in January if that you have a heated greenhouse, or February for harvests to be planted out in an unheated greenhouse. If utilizing a windowsill sow from late February for open-air development, sow inside toward the beginning of March.

Plants are currently broadly-offered available to be purchased in greenhouse focuses and are perfect where plant raising is troublesome. Joined plants have great energy and appropriate to cooler conditions and for soil development.

Develop

Despite the fact that aubergines can be developed outside, they infrequently well with the exception of in mellow territories or during awesome summers. Therefore they are better grown in a greenhouse or developing casing.

Develop in 9cm (3½in) pots at first, and when the pot is loaded up with attaches move plants to 23cm (9in) pots of manure in April in a heated greenhouse, early May if unheated or the finish of May or early June if developing outside.

Aubergines can likewise be developed in the open ground, in heat pieces of Britain, dividing 60cm (2ft) separated, and in a perfect world covering with cloches or wool. The keys to progress are daylight and heat, developing conditions. Heat the dirt with polythene or cloches two weeks before planting once there is no peril of ice and spread young plants in cloches or frames for a further two weeks until acclimatized. Develop them in a shielded, radiant position, in a perfect world against a heat, protected divider.

Stake and tie in plants as they develop. At the point when plants are 30cm (12in) high, expel the tip from the primary stem.

Water regularly and feed with a high potassium fluid manure like clockwork once the first organic product has set. Mist the foliage consistently (in any event twice every day) to with lukeheat water to demoralize red creepy-crawly parasite and help natural product set.

Evacuate remaining blossoms when five or six natural products have set. Cultivars creating little or round natural product can be permitted to deliver some more.

Chapter Nine: Scheduling Plants For Year-Round

Market greenhouse workers attempt to plan their planting so they can offer clients a constant inventory of new blossoms, herbs, and vegetables all through the developing season. This distribution assists cultivators with arranging planting times and progression planting.

The best way to deal with getting ready for a ceaseless collect is to keep acceptable creation records from past developing seasons and to contrast notes and other neighbourhood cultivators. You likewise can discover information in seed indexes and Extension announcements.

You have to know, or have the option to gauge:

- appropriate planting dates

- number of days to gather

- length of gather from first to last pickings

These elements are influenced by a few things. Climate, for instance, is a significant variable. Suitable planting dates are ordinarily booked around the standard yearly ice-free period in the spring and the usual annual first-freeze time in the fall. You can get these dates for your territory from your nearby Extension specialist or greenhouse store.

Climate affects timing as a result of its impact on seedling build up crop development. For instance, peas planted at the first conceivable planting date in the spring and afterwards again two weeks after the fact will typically develop just a single week separated. Germination conditions at the time planting will probably be significantly improved, and the young plants will become quicker as the days stretch, gradually finding the primary crop. This equivalent procedure occurs backward for fall crops. Indeed, even a few days' distinctions in midsummer planting dates can lead to a collect date distinction of two, or even three, weeks.

Two different ways to broaden the collect time frame for specific crops are 1) to plant assortments with an alternate number of days to development simultaneously, and 2) to plant a similar assortment on various occasions in progression.

Sweet corn frequently is developed in successive plantings to draw out the gathering season. A decent method to amaze sweet corn plantings is to hold up until one harvest is 1 to 2 inches tall before planting the following. Sweet corn will grow in general rise all the more gradually in cool soil (50–55°F) than in heat soil (68–77°F). Standard sweet corn assortments are preferable for

CROP	seed to flat, planned	seed to flat, actual	plant to the field, planned	plant to the field, actual	Estimated days to harvest	actual days to harvest	length of harvest	interval between plantings	comments

late-winter plantings over the super-sweet assortments since the super-sweet assortments won't also proceed in cool soil. Planting sweet corn around a multi-week before the asserted age ice-free date is a general guideline for the earliest plantings. On the last part of the planting season, make your last planting around 80 days before the usual first fall ice date. Notwithstanding successive plant-ings, you can plant assortments that require various time allotments to arrive at development. For instance, some sweet corn assortments are reproduced to develop in 70 days, while others require 100 days.

Planting as per ideal soil temperature is another usual method to plan plantings. The table underneath, Soil temperature Germination Ranges for Select Vegetables, gives a quick synopsis.

Soil Temperature Germination Ranges for Select Vegetables	
TEMP (°F)	PLANT
45–85	cabbage, kale, broccoli, collards (germinate well at 85, seedlings prefer 45–65)
35–80	lettuce and most salad greens (at more than 80, the germination rate drops 50%)
35–75	spinach (optimum 68)
50–85	onions (optimum 75)
45–95	radishes (optimum 85)
50–85	beets, Swiss chard (optimum 85)
60–85	beans snap and dry (optimum 80)
70–85	beans, lima (optimum 85)
40–75	peas (optimum 75)
60–95	corn (optimum 95)
65–82	tomatoes (optimum 80)
60–95	peppers (optimum 85)
65–100	cucumbers, melons, squash (optimum 80–95)

Bugs and infections are another primary consideration that can influence creation scheduling. In the muggy southeast, tomato developers regularly plant both spring and fall tomato crops on the grounds that the early plants surrender to infection in mid-summer. A market plant specialist in North Carolina reports that she sets out tomatoes multiple times during the developing season. She likewise noticed that squash vine borer is so awful in summer squash that she just gets around about fourteen days of reap from each planting.

When you have a design of conceivable individual arrangement for successive plantings, the Succession Planting graph, on the following page, can be utilized as a layout and adjusted for your area.

Succession Planting

arugula					30			2 weeks	best in cool weather
beans, bush					60			2 weeks	summer
beans, lima					65			*	summer
beans, pole					60-70			*	summer
beets					40-70			2 weeks	spring & fall
broccoli					60-70 f.t.			2 weeks	spring & fall
cabbage					70-80 f.t.			3 weeks	spring & fall
carrots					85-95			3 weeks	spring & fall
cauliflower					50-65 f.t.			2 weeks	spring & fall
collards					60-100			*	fall
corn, sweet					70-100			2 weeks	summer
cucumbers					60			4-5 weeks	summer
edamame					70			*	summer
eggplants					65 f.t.			8 weeks	summer
kale					40-50			2 weeks	spring & fall
kohlrabi					50-60			2 weeks	spring & fall
lettuce, head					70-85			2 weeks	spring & fall
lettuce, leaf					40-50			2 weeks	best in cool weather
muskmelons					80-90			2 weeks	summer
okra					70			*	summer
onions, dry					90-120 f.t.			*	
onions, green					85			2-3 weeks	
greens					30-60			2 weeks	best in cool weather
peas					55-70			*	spring & fall
peas, southern					65			*	summer
peppers					60-70 f.t.			*	summer
potatoes					90			*	spring & fall
pumpkins					90-120			*	summer
radishes					25-30			2 weeks	best in cool weather
radishes, daikon					60-75			*	spring & fall
spinach					50-60			2 weeks	spring & fall
squash, summer					45-60			4-8 weeks	summer
squash, winter					90-120			*	summer
tomatoes					65-90 f.t.			2	summer
turnips					35-40			2 weeks	best in cool weather

Chapter Ten: Growing Hoophouse/Greenhouse Hoophouse

A greenhouse permits the producer to control the temperature and condition inside a particular range so as to upgrade temperatures for top development consistently.

Staying with this acknowlframed standard, a simple method to make the qualification between the two designs is that a high passage utilizes inactive ventilation for air trade and cooling. On the other hand, a greenhouse is typically furnished with power and has mechanized heating and ventilation frameworks – more on this underneath. Be that as it may, remember this when attempting to disclose the distinction to another person: High passage = latent. Greenhouse = dynamic. This is a simple seeing, however, normally a supportive hop-off point.

The key term here is as a rule. To an ever-increasing extent, these two alternatives are covering and advancing with the requirements of producers. Be that as it may, with the end goal of this blog, we will pass by the generally tolerating meanings of every one of these choices.

The Similarities

The two choices are utilized to expand developing seasons. Frequently, a high passage is being used for "season expansion" while a greenhouse can be used for four-season developing. Both assist producers with beginning prior in spring and develop long into the cooler, darker long periods of pre-winter.

Since there is no mechanized heating or ventilation in a high passage, they are utilized predominantly in progressively calm locales to expand temperature in late-winter, fall, and in some cases, winter. Once more, this relies upon your area and furthermore what crops you decide to develop.

However, both high passages and greenhouses likewise offer some benefit in increasingly tropical locales by protecting harvests from unnecessary precipitation. Decreased dampness implies diminished odds of damaging ailments, for example, Phytophthora root spoil. For anybody that has ever lost a collect to this ruinous illness, presenting support between your plants (and work or nourishment source) and the components can't be downplayed.

How do these designs secure your plants? Every alternative is additionally canvassed in a coating – or material used to shield your harvests from the different ecological and vermin related rivals examined before. These will change between the alternatives and are clarified in more detail beneath.

And keeping in mind that the acknowlframed standard is that high passages are the less "connected" variant of developing designs, both can be outfitted with heating and ventilation frameworks.

The Differences

Think about a high passage as a crossbreed of a greenhouse and open field developing choice. Your crops are shielded from the components and other dangerous powers, for example, untamed life and hurtful, creepy crawlies, however, are not in a totally shut space similarly as with a greenhouse. For obviously characterizing what isolates a high passage from a greenhouse, this area will be more thorough than The Similarities.

Sturdiness

Similarly, as a high passage shields your harvests from components, for example, plunging evening temperatures, unsuitable presentation to rain, and dangerous wind loads, a greenhouse will furnish a similar worth yet frequently with a more significant level of sturdiness. The additional advantage is the capacity to take on greater discipline from wind and from the heaviness of day off, likewise to keep out the virus even profound into the coldest Alaskan winters.

COST

With the additional strength and season-broadening ability, comes an uptick in price. There are high passages that are more costly than greenhouses; however, it is protected to accept that high passages offer a lower cost for every square foot than you can anticipate from a greenhouse. In any case, with the capacity to develop all year, it is conceivable to balance those additional expenses with an additional period of producing income.

HOW CROPS ARE PLANTED

With a greenhouse, plants are developed on seats, raised bed units, or hydroponically. In a high passage, crops are regularly grown legitimately in the dirt or in raised beds.

VENTILATION AND HEATING

While there are covering choices as far as heating and ventilation, the acknowlframed standard is that a greenhouse comes outfitted with these alternatives and a high passage takes into consideration this choice in explicit cases. And keeping in mind that each will have a coating that covers the design, a greenhouse is made of polycarbonate, glass, or twofold layer film and a high passage is typically canvassed in a single layer film. We talk about the different coating alternatives in a past post for those that desire to all the more likely comprehend their choices.

Ventilation in a high passage is commonly moved upsides and large open entryways at each finish of the passage. At the point when these openings are shut, sun oriented heatth develops inside the design during the daytime and can keep it heat as the night progressed. Obviously, this won't serve producers very well in strength zones 1-4 where evening temperatures fall well underneath freezing with little daylight during the day. A greenhouse is increasingly helpful right now ventilation is typically an assortment of fans, pipes, and vents to advance the earth through a mechanized natural control framework.

Chapter Twelve: Hydroponics In A Greenhouse

The hydroponic greenhouse has the innovation and frameworks essential for the framework of a culture dependent on the standards of hydroponics, which can be characterized as:

Water system framework by which the root crops are adjusted supplement arrangement broke down in the water with all the synthetic concoctions essential for the development of plants, which can be developed straightforwardly on the mineral arrangement, or in a substrate or medium idle.

So we can recognize distinctive cultivating frameworks that exist in hydroponics:

Fluid medium in hydroponic systems:

These frameworks have not substrates for the improvement of crops, which happens legitimately on the water-bearing frameworks by different plants as:

Profound Flow Hydroponics: NGS.

Skimming frameworks: Floating Shelves.

Frameworks by water profundity: NFT.

Aeroponic frameworks:

A few designs remain the foundation of the way of life out, in a holder that keeps her out of the loop, where the supplement arrangement as a Mist splash is applied.

Frameworks hydroponic substrate:

In these frameworks, latent substrates flooded by a dribble water system, sub-irrigation, or overflowing are utilized for development. The most widely recognized substrates are perlite, rock wool, coconut fiber and peat.

Seats or furrows crops.

Sack developing.

Developing in singular holders or channels.

Surface harvest (sanded).

Thusly, the hydroponic frameworks could be arranged by the utilization of water they have, so we find:

Shut frameworks:

In these frameworks, a distribution of the supplement arrangement happens. They require a purification procedure for new application recycled. The sterilization frameworks are the most widely recognized use of sodium hypochlorite, chlorine dioxide or hypochlorous corrosive, ozone and light radiation.

Open frameworks or misfortune arrangement:

These frameworks discarded channels from the ranch.

Advantages of hydroponic in a greenhouse:

- Keep up ideal conditions for most magnificent photosynthetic execution.
- Amplifies vitality use from photosynthesis to build the crop of harvests.
- It improved water use.
- More space proficient: The surface prerequisites are less for a similar creation than traditional developing.
- Abbreviates crop cycles. Plant development is quicker.
- Take care of issues brought about by soil exhaustion: Facilitating the utilization of work.
- Resolve the issues created by soil exhaustion.

Chapter Thirteen: Managing And Operating A Greenhouse Pest And Diseases

Numerous specialists state that a productive greenhouse depends on the making of an Integrated Pest Management (IPM) program. An IPM program utilizes an assortment of strategies and systems to forestall, screen, and control bugs. These projects ought to be as least perilous as conceivable to people, property, and the earth.

While making your IPM, Greenhouse Management Magazine suggests that you consider the accompanying components that add to the upkeep of a malady and irritation-free greenhouse:

PLANT VULNERABILITY

As per greenhouse crop experts, you should know when your crops are progressively vulnerable to illness. From mold and rusts to infections and root decays, the malady can unleash destruction on your plants. It's critical to comprehend the indications of the most well-known ailments so you can appropriately plan for and treat the conditions.

Plant pros likewise propose that you become mindful of the kinds of bugs that might be pulled in to explicit plant species. To forestall malady, it is prescribed that you lead exhaustive research on the unfavourable irritations that might be generally attracted to your crops. The absolute most normal greenhouse bugs include:

- **Aphids (Plant Lice)** — The little, drowsy creepy crawlies bunch in states and tend to duplicate quickly. Bended stems and leaves are basic when they're available.
- **Organism Gnats** — While grown-ups can be found on foliage, hatchlings tunnel in the dirt and will benefit from root hairs, making the plant wither or become less enthusiastically. At the point when fully developed, these gnats have little bodies with long legs and clear wings.
- **Shore Flies** — These flies are like organism gnats however have shorter receiving wires, red eyes, darker bodies, and smoky wings. They can be watched laying on any surface in the greenhouse and have been known to spread soil pathogens inside yards.
- **Bloodworms** — Boasting a conspicuous red shading, these worms have long bodies and no legs. They visit regions with standing water or over the top dampness and will benefit from any green growth or natural issue.
- **Thrips** — These minor creepy crawlies have four wings and a column of long hairs. They are generally found on the plant surface or leaves, and they feed on any radiating sap.

They will in general assault azalea, calla lily, cyclamen, cucumber, fuschia, ivy, and rose plants.

- **Whiteflies** — A progressively perilous irritation, whiteflies are regularly impervious to bug sprays and require close observing to annihilate from greenhouses. They have white, fine bodies and are frequently seen under leaves of fuchsia, poinsettia, cucumber, lettuce, and tomato plants.

- **Leafminers** — These nuisances start harming plants as hatchlings, nourishing between the external surfaces of leaves. The leaves will turn light in shading and thin as invasion increments and hatchlings develop. Once completely developed, the hatchlings transform into flies that addition eggs into pits in leaf surfaces. Lamentably, since a large portion of the phases of development happens inside leaves, bug sprays aren't valuable at executing or expelling leafminers. Hand expulsion and removal of infected leaves are suggested.

- **Mealybugs** — Small and delicate bodied mealybugs feed on plant sap and produce honeydew that makes a shape on leaves and stems. They're frequently observed assaulting croton plants, hoyas, and bamboo palms.

- **Two-spotted Spider Mites** — These irritations have two dark specks on their mid-regions, making them simpler to recognize. They feast on sap on the underside of leaves, bringing about a spotted, yellow, or dry leaf appearance. If that a pervasion is extreme, the plants might be shrouded in a fine webbing that is created by the vermin. They are attracted toward marigolds, crotons, chrysanthemums, roses, impatiens, parlour palms, bamboo palms, and ivy.

- **Cyclamen Mites** — Small and semi-straightforward in nature, these bugs can assault whole plants or simply the plant buds. They can be seen on African violets, cyclamen, dahlia, and gloxinia. At the point when a pervasion happens, plant leaves become mutilated or twisted.

- **Slugs and Snails** — These vermin are pulled in to high-mugginess atmospheres and incessant leaves, stems, blossoms, and roots. Openings in leaves are generally observed with an invasion.

Greenhouse SANITATION

Many experienced greenhouse cultivators have discovered that keeping up a spotless greenhouse will permit you to give more consideration to your crops over the developing season. To guarantee a smooth and beneficial developing season, it's prescribed that producers play out these errands:

1. Force wash floors, dividers, gear, and different surfaces.

2.Clean floors, dividers, and water system hardware to forestall future greenhouse illness and pervasion.

3. Clean pots that you plan on reusing in a fade.

4. Evacuate weeds.

5. Investigate shades and covers for indications of wear and maturing.

6. Discard junk and old pesticides.

7. Check hardware to ensure everything is running appropriately.

Utilizing BIOLOGICAL CONTROL (BIOCONTROL) AGENTS

Regular and gainful creatures, known as natural control specialists, can be acquainted with your greenhouse to ward off and forestall pervasion. As indicated by a report by the NC State University Department of Entomology, living beings' adequacy can rely upon numerous elements including the atmosphere, conceptive rates, bug life cycles, and the number of nuisances included. Because of the enormous scope of items, further research ought to be led to explicit pests being focused.

Biocontrol specialists help to control pervasion normally, yet it sets aside effort for the operators to scatter and look for prey. Because of the deferral, it's prescribed that specialists be discharged whenever there's any hint of bugs in a greenhouse. If that your greenhouse is as of now vigorously plagued, specialists prompt utilizing an insecticidal cleanser or non-leftover bug spray on harvests to lessen the number of irritations before the arrival of biocontrol operators. Nonetheless, it's critical to remember that bug spray medicines ought to be constrained. Harvest authorities alert that if an excessive number of medications are utilized, the natural control operators may not be successful.

How about we investigate some natural control specialists that are usually used to dispose of greenhouse bugs:

Predictable ENVIRONMENT

Since numerous bugs and infections flourish in hot and sticky situations, temperature and mugginess are urgent to the accomplishment of greenhouses. Specialists propose that a single direction to control heat and dampness is by using a characteristic ventilation framework. These frameworks permit outside air to move over the width of greenhouses, supporting in temperature and stickiness control, air course, and CO_2/oxygen substitution.

The outside breeze can profit plants through transpiration and cell divider fortifying, assisting with keeping them stable. In the interim, steady air development makes uniform conditions all through the whole greenhouse. With calm conditions, greenhouse problem areas are cleared out, and high mugginess rates are brought down and managed, ending the reproducing reason for vermin and malady.

Observing and RECORD-KEEPING

A youthful research understudy with a tablet PC in a greenhouse Michigan State University AgBio Research report shows that crop watching is essential with regards to keeping up a fruitful greenhouse. It's prescribed that all cultivators draw up an arrangement or plan for a request to intently see specific segments or lines of their greenhouse each and every day. To investigate plants, you should turn leaves over and check for staining. The report additionally asks cultivators to expel plants from their pots and assess pulls for indications of root pathogens. While examining, you ought to be vigilant for:

- Spotted or twisted foliage or blossoms
- Creepy crawlies
- Creepy crawly skins
- Pockets of kicking the bucket plants
- Strange development or conduct

Moreover, it's recommended that you place yellow, blue, or white clingy traps at the plant level to check for action and recognize vigorously plagued territories. Explicit hues help in the fascination of specific creepy crawlies. The yellow snares pull in thrips, whiteflies, organism gnats, and winged aphids, while the blue-shaded snares, for the most part, attract thrips. White snares can help distinguish parasite gnats as fully-developed grown-ups. Greenhouse Management Magazine prescribes using in any event one to two cards for every 500 to 1,000 square feet. The cards ought to be supplanted week after week.

For enormous scope the executives of nuisances, Greenhouse Canada proposes the utilization of long clingy tapes to pull in and catch bugs. They will help lessen pervasion, giving you more command over your greenhouse condition.

While treating your greenhouse for malady and irritations, it's encouraged to put pointers in spots where there is an invasion. You can likewise utilize shaded stakes to pots to demonstrate if any plants have been showered with development controllers, bug sprays, or fungicides.

Utilizing AUTOMATION TO PREVENT GREENHOUSE INFESTATION AND DISEASE Suctioned Humidity Sensor Installed

A current rendition of conventional, manual greenhouses, mechanized greenhouses take into account expanded atmosphere control to help and secure crops. With the execution of engines, sensors, and interface boxes, numerous everyday greenhouse upkeep undertakings can happen consequently without the help of cultivators.

Computerized atmosphere controllers electronically control greenhouse parts like vent engines and blind developments. When setting up with the ideal programming, atmosphere controllers guarantee a reliable temperature and stickiness, assisting with discouraging the reproducing of bugs and infections.

Atmosphere control isn't the main advantage to greenhouse mechanization, however. Our computerized ventilation frameworks use:

Predominant RELIABILITY

With our lightweight, high torque, low voltage engines, drapery frameworks work with less moving parts and space prerequisites than practically identical frameworks. This guarantees less mechanical issues after some time.

Easy QUALITY CONTROL

Ventilation frameworks, fans, and heaters can be associated with and constrained by one, simple to-utilize unit. Clocks and sensors, related to the programming, initiate segments to keep up the ideal greenhouse conditions, helping the productivity of the cultivator.

Expanded ENERGY EFFICIENCY

Because of the utilization of sun oriented controllers, greenhouses can be mechanized with vitality given by the sun. In addition to the fact that it helps to eliminate vitality costs, sun-powered additionally provides the additional alternative and accommodation of developing in greenhouses in remote areas.

By and large, greenhouses with mechanization are useful from various perspectives, including overseeing and forestalling plant vermin and malady. In case you're looking for an approach to decrease work, save money on vitality costs, and improve the strength of your crops, robotization might be the arrangement you've been sitting tight.

CPSIA information can be obtained
at www.ICGtesting.com
Printed in the USA
BVHW011046190421
605287BV00003B/326